The Nonprofit Board Member's Guide to
Lobbying and Advocacy

by Marcia Avner
Minnesota Council of Nonprofits

with Kirsten Nielsen

AMHERST H.
WILDER
FOUNDATION

SAINT PAUL,
MINNESOTA

We thank The David and Lucile Packard Foundation and the
Amherst H. Wilder Foundation for supporting the production of this publication.

The Amherst H. Wilder Foundation is one of the largest and oldest endowed human service and community development organizations in the United States. Since 1906, the Wilder Foundation has been providing health and human services that help children and families grow strong, the elderly age with dignity, and the community grow in its ability to meet its own needs.

We hope you find this book helpful! Should you need additional information about our services, please contact:

Wilder Center for Communities
Amherst H. Wilder Foundation
919 Lafond Avenue
Saint Paul, MN 55104
phone 651-642-4022

For more information about other Wilder Foundation publications, please see the back of this book or contact:

Wilder Publishing Center
Amherst H. Wilder Foundation
919 Lafond Avenue
Saint Paul, MN 55104
800-274-6024
www.wilder.org/pubs

Edited by Vincent Hyman
Text designed by Kirsten Nielsen
Cover designed by Rebecca Andrews

Manufactured in the United States of America

First printing, July 2004

Library of Congress Cataloging-in-Publication Data

Avner, Marcia, 1943-
   The nonprofit board member's guide to lobbying and advocacy / by Marcia Avner, with Kirsten Nielsen.
      p. cm.
   ISBN 0-940069-39-3
   1. Lobbying--United States--Handbooks, manuals, etc. 2. Lobbying--Law and legislation--United States--Handbooks, manuals, etc. I. Nielsen, Kirsten, 1974- II. Title.

JK1118.A98 2004
324'.4'0973--dc22
                              2004012581

About the Author

Marcia Avner is public policy director for the Minnesota Council of Nonprofits. At MCN she lobbies on behalf of the nonprofit sector, writes and speaks extensively, and provides training nationwide to support nonprofit boards, staff, and volunteers in their efforts to be effective advocates. She is also an assistant professor in the Master of Arts in Nonprofit Management Program at Hamline University, where she teaches advocacy and lobbying and on the faculty at the Center for Advocacy and Political Leadership at the University of Minnesota–Duluth.

Prior to her work with the Minnesota Council of Nonprofits, Marcia served as state communications director for U.S. Senator Paul D. Wellstone and worked with Sheila Wellstone to develop a national advocacy agenda for domestic violence prevention and intervention. She also served as deputy mayor of Saint Paul, executive director of The Minnesota Project, a nonprofit organization dedicated to rural community development, assistant commissioner for energy in the Minnesota Department of Trade and Economic Development, and legislative director for the Minnesota Public Interest Research Group.

She has served on more than twenty nonprofit boards and advisory committees, currently including Charity Lobbying in the Public Interest, Jewish Community Action, Lifetrack Resources, and Wellstone Action.

Marcia began her advocacy and lobbying work in 1972 when she served as president of the board of the Minneapolis Association for the Hearing Impaired. Like many board members who champion advocacy efforts, she was drawn to writing and speaking out in policy arenas on behalf of matters dear to heart: her own hearing-impaired son and all the families struggling with deafness. The work began a thirty-four-year journey of learning and advocating for nonprofit leadership in public policy efforts.

Acknowledgments

This book has been shaped by the many advocates who have served as my teachers, colleagues, and inspiration. It is also a response to the countless people who have worked with *The Lobbying and Advocacy Handbook for Nonprofit Organizations* and asked for specific ideas for board member leadership in advancing policy issues.

Many people shared their experience, stories, and expertise; without them, this book would not have been possible. Others provided helpful guidance by serving as field-test reviewers. For their enthusiasm, wisdom, and help, thanks to

- Audrey Alvarado, Executive Director, National Council of Nonprofit Associations
- Liz Baumgarten, Executive Director, Charity Lobbying in the Public Interest
- Tom Birch, Legislative Counsel, National Assembly of State Arts Agencies
- Sheri Brady, Policy Director, National Council of Nonprofit Associations
- Karen Diver, Former Board Chair, Minnesota Council of Nonprofits, Fond du Lac Reservation
- Marvin Eckfeldt, President of the Board of Trustees, King County Sexual Assault Center
- Dave Edwards, Board President, Washington State Historical Society
- Lynne Faltraco, Concerned Citizens of Rutherford County (CCRC)
- Denise Harlow, Director of Nonprofit Services, Council of Community Services of New York State (CCSNYS)

- Diane Hartz Warsoff, Utah Nonprofit Association
- Patricia Gardner, Executive Director, Silicon Valley Council of Nonprofits
- Gita Gulati-Partee, OpenSource Leadership Strategies
- Edie Kirkwood, Board Chair, Silicon Valley Council of Nonprofits
- Bill Malloy, Board Member, Center for Human Development
- David Maurrasse, Alliance for Nonprofit Management
- Larry Meyer, John S. and James L. Knight Foundation
- Layli Miller-Muro, Executive Director, Tahirih Justice Center
- Rebecca Lynn Petersen, Board Chair, Minnesota Citizens for the Arts
- Bill Sellars, Board Member, Arc of King County, Board Member at Large, Arc of Washington State
- Sarajane Siegfriedt, Board Secretary, Freemont Public Association
- Bob Smucker, Charity Lobbying in the Public Interest
- Scott Snow, Executive Director, Utah Commission on Volunteers– Office of the Lieutenant Governor
- Diane Trapani, Development Director, Interim, Inc.
- Alene Valkanis, Illinois Arts Alliance
- David zum Brunnen, Board President, Arts North Carolina

I would also like to thank Brian Buzby, Carolyn Cunningham, Carol Freeman, Liz Heath, Jonathan Lever, Joan Mobley, and Paula Wolf for their help in locating our wonderful storytellers.

Kirsten Nielsen and Vince Hyman at Wilder Publishing Center had a major role in the development of the book. Kirsten conducted interviews and edited the stories that make the key themes come to life. Vince inspired the concept for the publication and is the best editor an author could imagine. Both have my deepest gratitude and have made the work a user-friendly tool for advancing advocacy.

Additional thanks to Karen Diver, Fond du Lac Reservation, and Sarah Stoesz, Planned Parenthood of Minnesota and the Dakotas, who served as board chairs at the Minnesota Council of Nonprofits while this work was being developed. The Board of Directors and the Public Policy Cabinet of the Minnesota Council of Nonprofits make advocacy and lobbying a high priority and are involved in advocacy and lobbying planning and activity. They provide a model for organizational leadership.

Jon Pratt, MCN's Executive Director, has championed the vision of the nonprofit sector as a leading force in shaping public policy. He and other members of the MCN Policy Team—Nan Madden, Christina Macklin, and Elena Doucet-Beer—have been instrumental in doing model nonprofit policy work.

Thanks to MCN legislative intern Max Cecil for his assistance with manuscript preparation.

Wyman Spano, my partner and mentor, shares my commitment to encouraging nonprofit advocacy and ensuring that people who are affected by policy decisions have a voice in shaping policy. He inspires and supports my work and this writing.

Support from the Otto Bremer Foundation, the McKnight Foundation, the Minneapolis Foundation, the Jay and Rose Phillips Foundation, and the David and Lucille Packard Foundation was essential to the development of this book.

United States Senator Paul Wellstone often said, "The future will belong to those who have passion, and to those who are willing to make the personal commitment to make our country better." I am ever grateful to Sheila and Paul Wellstone, Tom Lapic, and Mary McEvoy for the example they set and the lessons they taught: choosing to speak out on issues we care about can shape policies that improve people's lives.

Dedication

This book is dedicated to you, the thousands of individuals who give their talents and time to serve on boards of nonprofit organizations. Without your leadership, nonprofits would not be the vital force they have always been in American society.

With your encouragement and involvement, nonprofit organizations will continue to build their capacity in public policy work. Through advocacy and lobbying, you will advance your organization's mission, causes, and issues. Your involvement is a critical factor in determining the impact and success of your nonprofit's public policy strategy. And public policies set the context, and sometimes the funding, for how effectively your nonprofit can provide the programs and services that you care about in your communities.

Be involved in advancing advocacy and lobbying. The nonprofit organizations you support depend on you to help them be effective agents of change.

Contents

Lobbying by charities is often the best service they can provide. Government plays a large role in funding services that are provided by charities, and government often has substantial control over programs offered by nonprofits. It follows that one important role, if not the most important role, of a charity board member is to use his or her influence to lobby for legislation that will further the charity's service objectives.

—Bob Smucker, Founder, Charity Lobbying in the Public Interest

Introduction

Nonprofit organizations can and should participate in shaping public policy through advocacy and lobbying. Consider that public policy is the set of decisions that we make about how we will care for one another. In our democracy, nonprofits have been an effective voice in shaping policies that improve people's lives and the places where they live. Policies also create and change the framework in which nonprofits work. By helping to create supportive policies, nonprofits strengthen their ability to fulfill their own missions.

Board members have a critical role to play in an organization's efforts to shape public policies at the local, state, and federal level. As a board member you may already be involved in your nonprofit organization's advocacy efforts to build awareness of community needs and the ways in which your organization solves community problems. It is nonprofits that have built awareness of such issues as the need for affordable housing, the importance of early childhood development strategies, the benefits of recycling precious resources, and the impact of prevention and early intervention strategies to address violence in our society.

Lobbying is a specific and important component of your nonprofit's ongoing advocacy efforts. Through lobbying, your organization can identify and press for adoption of specific laws and regulations that will further your organization's mission. It is also exciting and rewarding work! It is your opportunity to shape and sustain public policies that reflect your organization's values and priorities.

How Do Board Members Contribute?

There are four essential and unique ways in which board members contribute to advocacy and lobbying for nonprofits; three of those relate to the board's key role in governing the organization, and one to the board's investment as volunteers for the organization.

1. As *governors* for the organization, board members participate in and enrich strategic planning for public policy work.

2. Also in their governance role, board members determine the strategic direction and priorities for the organization's public policy advocacy and lobbying work. They allocate resources to advocacy and lobbying, set the organizational policy for how resources are raised, and often assist in fundraising efforts.

3. Also in their governance role, board members are responsible for the legal obligations of the organization, including accurate recording and reporting of lobbying activity, filing of the appropriate forms, and staying within the lobbying expenditure limits.

4. As *volunteers* for the organization, board members advocate and lobby (the fun part)!

As a board member, you have volunteered to serve an organization that you believe does important work in your community. Your organization provides you the opportunity to contribute to work that furthers your personal vision of a better society. By definition, you as a board member are

- A community leader, representing community interests
- A volunteer prepared to dedicate time and resources to meeting your nonprofit organization's mission
- A key stakeholder in the organization's success and sustainability
- A champion for the organization's approach to solving community problems
- A steward of the organization, well versed in its mission, goals, strategies, programs, and possibilities

Because you represent both your organization *and* the community your organization serves, you can be a powerful voice for your organization's policy positions. By virtue of your title and position, you have power and access to decision makers that your organization's staff and the people you serve may not have. Use this privilege to move your organization's work forward.

Who This Book Is For

The Nonprofit Board Member's Guide to Lobbying and Advocacy is for you, the board member of a nonprofit organization that wants to increase its impact on policy decisions. The two primary strategies included in this book—planning and action—are designed to meet the needs of all types of nonprofit boards. Whether your nonprofit is large, midsized, or small; whether it is national or local in focus; whether it is committed to human services, arts, environmental, educational, human rights, or health issues; whether your nonprofit is experienced or a rookie at lobbying, this book is for you.

The concepts, principles, and strategies in this book will be helpful to all nonprofit leaders but are specifically intended for board members of 501(c)(3) charities. Choose the components that suit your unique situation.

How to Use This Book

This book can be used alone or as a companion to *The Lobbying and Advocacy Handbook for Nonprofit Organizations.*[1] That handbook is an in-depth planning guide and resource for nonprofit boards and staff. It includes an eight-step planning process for building an organization's strategic plan and capacity to sustain its work in advocacy and lobbying. It also includes detailed guidance in effective lobbying at the state and local level.

---

[1] *The Lobbying and Advocacy Handbook for Nonprofit Organizations,* by Marcia Avner, is available from the Amherst H. Wilder Foundation. (800-274-6024, www.wilder.org/pubs)

If your organization is building its readiness for integrating advocacy and lobbying into its overall efforts, *The Lobbying and Advocacy Handbook for Nonprofit Organizations* can facilitate that organizational process. At the same time, this book can provide specific support to board members for their role in planning and in being an influential voice for the organization.

Using this book, you, the board member, will

- Recognize that lobbying does further a nonprofit's mission and is a valuable—and legal—part of nonprofit work
- Understand your role in planning for your nonprofit's public policy work
- Work with your organization's staff to implement effective lobbying actions
- Identify ways in which you can tap your leadership status and personal strengths to contribute to lobbying efforts
- Build your own skills and effectiveness as a participant in your nonprofit's lobbying and media advocacy efforts

Let's begin!

CHAPTER 1

Advocacy and Lobbying
Key to Your Nonprofit Organization's Mission

As a nonprofit board member, you can and should advocate and lobby. It is a strategic way to use your position to advance your organization's cause. And contrary to what you may have heard, it is legal. This chapter examines the difference between advocacy and lobbying, the rationale for nonprofit involvement in public policy, and highlights of appropriate nonprofit lobby laws.

Why Lobby?

Lobbying builds policies that improve people's lives and the places where they live. Consider your nonprofit's mission. Recognize how important it is to have state and local laws, and sometimes public funding, in order to carry out programs and provide services. Without a supportive policy framework, nonprofits dedicated to all sorts of goals—housing, economic development, human rights, civic engagement, fair taxes—would not be able to accomplish their goals and meet their missions.

Nonprofits do a lot to promote the interests of their communities. Your organization most likely already does some form of advocacy work. You may be raising awareness of the value of literacy, fighting for livable wages, or encouraging recycling. Perhaps you advocate for victims in the criminal justice system or urge community planners to incorporate public art into their initiatives. Think of lobbying as a specific and critical component of the general advocacy that you already do to advance the issues that matter to you.

A Few Terms You Need to Know

Lobbying is a special and essential type of nonprofit *advocacy* that shapes *public policy* in *arenas of influence* at the local, state, and national levels.

Public policy

Public policy is the combination of goals, laws, rules, and funding priorities set by public officials that determine how government meets needs, solves problems, and spends public funds. Public policy is formally set by elected officials at the federal, state, and local levels primarily through the legislative process. Public policy objectives and programmatic goals are set in law. Tax policies and budgets are passed by legislative bodies, which set revenue and spending priorities at every level of government.

Advocacy

Advocacy involves identifying, embracing, and promoting a cause. Advocacy is an effort to shape public perception or to effect change that may or may not require changes in the law. Nonprofits engage in advocacy to influence broad discussions of public policy.

For example, advocates for ending domestic violence have worked to raise public awareness of domestic violence as a problem in society and to change the way governmental agencies deal with it. They have successfully urged medical and educational professionals to recognize the signs of violence and abuse and respond to them. They have educated police and emergency responders about ways to protect and support victims of violence. And they have coached and supported victims as they worked their way through the legal and social service systems in search of safety. These organizations have created change through measures that do not require changes in the law.

Lobbying

Lobbying is a form of advocacy specifically focused to influence legislation—specific laws that are formal statements of public policy. Nonprofits can urge legislators to pass laws and provide funds to solve a problem. Nonprofits can stop actions that would have negative impacts on issues and communities. For example, advocates for ending domestic violence have persuaded Congress to pass the federal Violence Against Women Act, city councils to pass local ordinances requiring mandatory arrests of domestic violence perpetrators, and state legislatures to pass mandatory sentences. These same advocates have lobbied in support of state and local budgets that provide funding for shelters for victims of violence, for antiviolence media campaigns, and for public assistance for victims moving from abusive situations to self-sufficiency.

Arenas of influence

Arenas of influence are those places where public policy is decided. Lobbying is most often targeted toward arenas of legislative activity: Congress, state legislatures, county commissions, city councils, school boards, and other local or regional entities. The administrative (or executive) branch of government is also an arena where changes are made through executive order, through changes in rules or administrative practices, and through the use of the veto by elected executives: the president, governor, or mayor. The courts (the judicial branch) make some policy decisions, and a number of nonprofits have had a profound impact on policy through litigation. Your organization's planning involves targeting the arenas where your issues will be decided and where your involvement can make the biggest difference.

Why Lobby?

Lobbying is a great way to advance your issues. It is legal, energizing, safe, and fun!

Because any advocacy campaign can include direct lobbying, community organizing and mobilizing, and even some media efforts, it taps the talents of a wide array of your supporters. Working together in campaigns that support good ideas or avert disasters, your organization can involve many people in meaningful activities all for the sake of advancing your cause.

Most of all, lobbying is one important strategy for ensuring that your work is adequately supported and that laws and rules support the programs and services that are your reason for existing!

Turn the Personal into the Political

Having a daughter with Down syndrome led me into the field of public policy work. I became a board member of Arc of King County because I wanted to make sure that my community had the services and opportunities my daughter needed. And I felt I might as well lobby for all individuals with developmental disabilities at the same time I was advocating for her needs. Arc's introduction of Citizen Lobbyists and Self-Advocates as vehicles of advocacy to legislative bodies has proven to be incredibly powerful.

When the Citizen Lobbyists of the Arc successfully lobbied for funding that provides employment and training in the transition from high school to work (Education for All), my daughter benefited; she was taught in integrated settings and has been employed for twelve years as an office assistant in the corporate headquarters of a large natural foods cooperative where she works twenty-four hours a week. Her pay is nominal, but she receives full medical and dental benefits, vacation time, sick time, and a 401(K) retirement plan. Her income allows her to live rather independently in shared housing with four

other young adults who have different developmental disabilities. But the funding that we lobbied for also created a whole group of working taxpayers whose jobs and incomes pay for their housing, clothing, health care, transportation, continuing education, and leisure activities. People who complete this sort of transitional training have jobs that last ten, fifteen, and twenty years or longer. They are reliable workers who rarely miss a day of work. Their presence boosts the morale and productivity of the workplace. In King County we now have 276 organizations that hire persons with developmental disabilities. Not only do disabled workers benefit, but employers, coworkers, and taxpayers benefit as well.

The experiences I've had in public policy have proved to me over and over again that a handful of people can make a tremendous difference. After all, it was four mothers and one law student who brought Education for All (now called IDEA) to our nation.

— *Bill Sellars, Board Member of the Arc of King County, Board Member at Large of the Arc of Washington State*

The Positive Impact of Nonprofit Lobbying

Much good has come from the lobbying efforts of nonprofit organizations. Consider the following:

- Nonprofit organizations that work to eradicate poverty have led many states to pass earned income tax credit legislation. These measures ensure that people who work have a better chance of maintaining income levels that will support themselves and their families.

- Countless seniors have been able to live independently even as they have grown frail because nonprofit organizations have lobbied for programs like meals on wheels, senior companion, and congregate dining. Funding for these programs keeps seniors in their homes and is much less expensive than options such as assisted living and nursing home care. Nonprofits whose mission is to maximize seniors' independence and quality of life can work within a policy context that supports their mission.

- Nonprofit community development corporations have lobbied for housing and planning laws and for budget appropriations that support well-designed, highly functional communities. They have helped to pass laws that enable them to meet their mission and provide a range of integrated housing options to community residents.

- Nonprofits that address health care needs have lobbied successfully for clean air and clean water legislation resulting in a healthier environment. The boards of these organizations know that their core mission is supported by working for societal standards that demand a healthy environment.

It's Legal!!!!

Countless nonprofits (and their boards) have backed away from lobbying out of fear. There is a common myth that it is illegal, or that if legal, it is risky. Neither is true! Congress has made it clear that nonprofits can lobby. In fact, Congress encourages nonprofits to lobby—it is a key role that nonprofits play in addressing the needs and interests of their constituents.

Nonprofit Lobbying: Worthy and Legal

Not only is lobbying a key strategy that nonprofits use to meet their mission, it is legal—in fact, Congress encourages nonprofits to lobby.

As a board member, you are responsible for your organization's compliance with laws regarding lobbying. Fortunately, Congress has made it clear that nonprofits are not only legally entitled to lobby, they are expected to do so. The 1976 Lobby Law makes very clear that nonprofits have a role in society that *includes* being a voice on issues that matter to people, communities, and the nation. So lobby, but do it legally. Follow the laws that govern the ways in which nonprofits must report and limit their lobbying expenditures.

The following section explains the laws that govern how much your 501(c)(3) is allowed to spend on lobbying, how to track your lobbying activity for reporting purposes, and how to report your lobbying to the Internal Revenue Service as part of your organization's annual filing of IRS Form 990. Additional information is in Appendix B.

The 1976 Lobby Law

Before 1976, there was enormous ambiguity over the amount of lobbying that nonprofits could do. The IRS rules required that tax-exempt nonprofits, 501(c)(3) organizations, lose their tax-exempt status if they did more than an "insubstantial" amount of lobbying. This "insubstantial-lobbying test" was never specifically defined in IRS rules, and individual IRS agents had no guidance in what constituted "too much lobbying." The vague guidelines were confusing to regulators and left nonprofits with great uncertainty about how much lobbying was legal—and may be the cause of the still widely held myth that nonprofits are prohibited from lobbying.

A law passed in 1976 clarified that nonprofits *can* lobby. Now nonprofits need to know how much lobbying is legal.

The 1976 Lobby Law establishes clear guidelines for lobbying expenditures. These guidelines are called the "lobbying-expenditure test" and were passed under Sections 501(h) and 4911 of the Tax Reform Act of 1976. This law clarifies that 501(c)(3) nonprofits that elect to fall under these rules

State Lobbying Laws

Be sure that your organization contacts the office of the attorney general and the office of the secretary of state to learn about lobbyist registration and reporting requirements in your state. Most states require all lobbyists, including nonprofit lobbyists, to report lobbying expenditures, and states often require nonprofits to identify the issues on which they are active. The guidelines vary greatly from state to state.

can spend up to a defined percentage of their budget for lobbying without threatening their tax-exempt status. In 1990 the IRS published final rules on implementing the Lobby Law. Those rules make it clear that nonprofits should elect to be covered by the lobbying-expenditure test and not fall under the vague insubstantial-lobbying test. As a board member, be sure that your nonprofit knows that it can choose whether or not to fall under the 1976 Lobby Law. If you elect to be covered by the Lobby Law, you need to do two things:

1. Take formal steps to elect to fall under the 1976 guidelines (File a simple, one-page IRS Form 5768. Get this paperwork to the IRS!)

2. Know the lobbying limits

The steps you need to take to follow the guidelines are clear and simple. Details, including a chart that helps you understand the lobbying limits, are provided in Appendix B. Use that appendix to guide your due diligence in planning for and executing your nonprofit's public policy initiatives.

So it is true—nonprofits can and should lobby. It makes a difference. And it is legal. The following two chapters focus on ways in which board members can participate in nonprofit planning for public policy work and engage in lobbying on their nonprofit's issues.

CHAPTER 2

Board Planning for Advocacy
Capacity and Strategies

Responsibilities of governance demand that board members engage in planning, keeping their sights on the long-term course for their nonprofit, setting policies, and ensuring that the organization is strategic in the use of its resources and true to its mission. Usually board planning sessions are devoted to strategic purposes. Advocacy should be among those strategies. This chapter identifies a planning process for developing and sustaining your nonprofit's public policy work.

In the best of times, planning is a sustained process based on anticipation of changing needs and opportunities, driven by commitment to the nonprofit's mission, and focused on the long-term ability of the organization to meet its goals. In difficult times, when financial, political, or management challenges demand action, board members do emergency planning, adapting their organization's strategic plan to meet unexpected demands. Boards have proven that they can be responsive and creative in trying times.

Often, a crisis provokes nonprofits' engagement in public policy work. Many nonprofit organizations initially jump into advocacy and lobbying on a reactive, emergency basis in response to budget cuts, regulatory changes, or policy-shaping opportunities.

But to maximize the benefits of your nonprofit's advocacy efforts, board members and staff must work intentionally to integrate advocacy planning with the organization's strategic plan.

Two critical planning components fall within the board's jurisdiction:

1. *Capacity*: strategic planning ensures that the nonprofit organization has adequate resources, staffing, training, and systems to sustain policy work.

2. *Strategy*: strategic planning shapes the organization's ability to select its advocacy priorities and the strategies and tactics that maximize long-term effectiveness in policy arenas. Planning addresses key questions:

   - What are our public policy goals for the issues that affect the people we serve?

   - How will our organization carry out our lobbying work?

Planning addresses these questions and is one of the board's most important contributions to nonprofit advocacy.

Getting Involved in a Planning Process

The Lobbying and Advocacy Handbook for Nonprofit Organizations proposes a detailed eight-step planning process for nonprofit boards and staff. The text provides agendas for six planning meetings (and shorter options as well) that comprise a thorough, thoughtful, and energetic process. The eight planning steps are

1. Prepare the planning team

2. Articulate vision and goals for your public policy effort

3. Establish criteria and identify issues that are your organization's policy priorities

4. Target arenas of influence where your policy issues are decided

5. Choose strategies and tactics that advance your issues successfully

6. Design the organizational infrastructure to sustain policy work

7. Create a work plan for your nonprofit's policy, advocacy, and lobbying

8. Present the plan and urge its integration with your nonprofit's activities

Grow from Reactive to Proactive Policy Work

My husband and I moved to rural Rutherford County in 1979. We bought a small parcel of land and lived in our "little piece of heaven" for almost twenty years. In June 1995, our neighbor read a public notice in the local newspaper that some industry was planning to purchase a large amount of land a few miles from our house and asked that we attend a community meeting about this industry. I attended the meeting along with six or seven people at our community's firehouse. We learned that the industry was going to construct a high-capacity satellite wood chip mill. After the first meeting, we decided to host our own community meetings at the Union Mills Club House. Soon forty, sixty, and eighty people were showing up on Saturday mornings to discuss the issue at hand.

We eventually formed a community-based, nonprofit organization called the Concerned Citizens of Rutherford County (CCRC) as a method to organize community members and create dialogue about environmental issues. Our first effort was to keep the wood chip mill from being built in our community. We managed to keep the mill from being constructed for three years. That experience made us aware of a number of issues, and we learned that industries and large corporations have a profile they use when considering various locations. High-impact industries typically target poor, rural communities to build their facilities and tout the incentive of "more jobs." They often do not disclose or consider the environmental impact that their industry will have on the community. They may also appeal to local politicians to secure support and money without considering community injustices.

Over the past nine years, CCRC has developed an extensive network along with various strategies to address environmental issues. Now, if any members become aware of an issue or a piece of legislation that affects the environmental rights of our community, we put it on the agenda for our upcoming meeting. The board then decides whether to become involved in the issue and activates our policy committee (three or four members), who spearhead the advocacy work. The policy committee creates a strategic plan (a set of activities) and orchestrates the work.

CCRC has come a long way from reactive policy work to planning and implementing policy efforts. We have become a voice for communities throughout the Southeast and Appalachian regions by mentoring and partnering with other communities dealing with unsustainable forestry practices.

—Lynne Faltraco, Program Coordinator
and Advisor, Concerned Citizens of
Rutherford County, North Carolina

Board members have a unique and critical role to play in each step of planning. A quick review of what you can do in the eight steps identified on page 17 illustrates the board's importance.

Planning Step 1: Prepare the planning team

Board members and staff select a planning team and a coordinator who will prepare a proposal for the full board's review. The board names planning team participants and prepares a charge to the team, setting forth the objectives, expected outcomes, and decision-making processes. At its initial meeting, the planning team completes Worksheet 1: Public Policy Readiness Inventory (see Appendix A, page 61). This is an assessment of public policy readiness and prepares the team to think about ways in which the organization can build its existing strengths.

What are the board members' roles in Step 1?

- A board member may be the one who initiates a proposal for planning advocacy and policy work. Someone has to start the discussion about beginning or formalizing your nonprofit's commitment to policy work. You, the board member, can be the leader.

- The board debates the merits of engaging in public policy and makes critical decisions about how important this is to the nonprofit.

- Board members work together to reach agreement on the composition of the planning team, the overall planning process, and the selection of board members to serve on the team.

- Board members with interest, experience, or expertise serve on the planning team.

Planning Step 2: Articulate vision and goals

Step 2 provides an opportunity for inspiration and reflection. The planning team takes time to imagine what a strong and effective public policy effort would accomplish. The team reviews the organization's mission and reaffirms that public policy work will enhance the organization's ability to meet its mission.

The Planning Process at a Glance

Step	Role of the board
1. Prepare the planning team	· Initiate the process · Debate the merits of engaging in advocacy · Create a planning team · Design the planning process · Select board members for the planning team
	Role of board members on the planning team
2. Articulate vision and goals	· Decide how advocacy serves your mission · Develop advocacy mission, vision, and goals · Identify broad policy goals · Participate as stewards of the organization
3. Establish criteria, identify issues	· Use research prepared by staff · Access others in your network for research and information support · Add your knowledge and judgment
4. Target arenas of influence	· Learn about the arenas: legislatures, agencies, and more · Rely on your networks to learn how the system really works! · Educate the full board about what you learn
5. Choose strategies and tactics	· Know and enforce legal guidelines · Share your experience and expertise · Be innovative! Consider coalitions and allies · Choose strategies that match your nonprofit's culture and long-term interests
6. Design organizational infrastructure	· Help delineate clear roles for the board · Volunteer to work on advocacy and lobbying efforts · Share your community contacts, potential allies · Help design infrastructure systems · Decide how your organization will make decisions in a timely way · Decide on the structure of a policy committee if you choose to create one · Work to set realistic budgets and ways to raise resources
7. Create the work plan	· Inform and review staff efforts
8. Present the work plan	· Assist in presenting the plan to the full board, addressing ideas and concerns, and securing support to advance the work

The entire board needs to give thoughtful consideration to the proposal!

Then the team works to develop a vision specific to public policy work and identifies the broad goals for advocacy and lobbying efforts.

The team prepares a written record that includes the mission statement and a vision for public policy work. A vision expresses what your organization will look like in three to five years with a strong and effective public policy component in place. How will the people and communities you serve be helped by your public policy efforts? How will you increase your ability to provide programs and services?

Next the team identifies broad public policy goals. These might include strong relationships with policy shapers, working alliances with other organizations that share policy goals, adequate capacity to do effective policy work over the long term, and specific changes in rules, regulations, or funding.

As a board member on the planning team, you

- Attend the planning meetings, share experience and insights, and engage actively.
- Are vigilant in your role as a steward for the organization and its mission. In the planning process, board members serve the team well by continuously examining ideas about vision and goals in light of the mission. Advocacy and lobbying should enhance effectiveness without distracting the organization from its basic path.

Planning Step 3: Establish criteria and identify issues

Now the team moves from setting broad policy goals to establishing criteria for setting issue priorities. These criteria are helpful as the organization becomes increasingly active. Firm guidelines help the organization choose its battles! The criteria should be simple, mission focused, and few in number. Criteria might include intentions to work on

- Legislation that threatens your organization's survival or funding
- Legislation that involves issues in which you have unique and valuable information to contribute

- Legislation that presents an opportunity to involve people who will be affected by the outcomes in the policy dialogue, thus furthering civic engagement

- Legislation that strengthens your organization's program and funding

- Legislation that advances your issues in new and innovative ways

With criteria in place, the planning team can identify issues and decide how to use time, talents, and energy to address those issues. Choose to work on issues that require immediate attention as well as long-term policy work. For example, this year you might work to sustain state funding for your art-in-the-parks program, but over the long term you might want your state to commit 2 percent of investments in public buildings to public art.

The planning team identifies clear positions the organization will take on each of the issues proposed. Issues and positions on those issues are recorded for future board discussion.

As a board member on the planning team, you

- May rely on staff to conduct research for the issues selection process. Ask staff to prepare information on issues already in discussion in public policy arenas, on issues you anticipate will be introduced in future debates, and on issues your organization might choose to initiate. Once issues are on the table, research will identify existing models, related work by other organizations, and past efforts to advocate and lobby on those issues.

- Assist staff and other board members by introducing them to community leaders who are knowledgeable about the issues under consideration. Knowing who has expertise about an issue is important when deciding what issues to address. And building relationships with community leaders now will help if your nonprofit seeks strategic alliances in the future.

- Contribute what you know about issues.

- Are tough. Make sure that the planning team is both ambitious and realistic about what it can accomplish, clearly understands its unique niche in the public dialogue on your issues, and is true to your organization's mission.

- Are bold. Encourage the planning team to think about the leadership role that your nonprofit can play on critical issues, and be prepared to take that leadership position.

Planning Step 4: Target arenas of influence

Your nonprofit will be working to influence government decision makers in one or more of three arenas: the legislative, executive, and judicial branches of government. In this planning step, the team studies and determines where decisions will be made about your issues and how you can have an impact in one or more of those arenas. Most nonprofits target their work to legislative and executive (administrative) arenas at the national, state, or local level.

Once the arenas of influence are targeted, the team and others in the organization expand their knowledge of how the process works and the people in the process—decision makers, staff, advocates, the media. The planning team can learn a great deal by taking time to do a "treasure hunt" at the capitol or city hall (see the sidebar on page 55). This, along with information provided by government and through staff work, can rapidly advance your knowledge of the arenas of influence.

As a board member on the planning team, you

- Actively participate in the learning process as the planning team explores arenas of influence.

- Use your relationships with others in the community who are elected officials, lobbyists, and leaders to gain information about how the system really works. You have access to people and information that your organization cannot reach without your leadership.

- Encourage the planning team to think of ways to educate the full board and staff about what the team learns about issues, arenas of influence, and processes for effecting change. Once others in the organization discuss and adopt a plan, they will need information and training about things you learned during the planning effort.

Planning Step 5: Choose strategies and tactics

Your team has planned its position on priority issues and determined where to work for the desired results. There is a wide array of strategies your organization could use in its lobbying work. You choose the approaches that are most promising, given your priorities. Whether your arena of influence is the Congress or the county board, your nonprofit will be most effective if you use a two-pronged approach: direct lobbying and grassroots mobilizing.[2]

Direct lobbying is the action your organization takes to persuade elected and appointed officials to adopt your position and vote or act the way your organization wants them to on your issues.

Grassroots mobilizing involves educating and activating the public to persuade elected and appointed officials to support and act on your positions on issues.

Nonprofits have two primary sources of power: valuable information and the voices of people who care about the nonprofit's issues. Direct lobbying and grassroots mobilizing enable nonprofits to use those two sources of power effectively.

See Worksheet 2: Lobbying Strategies, in Appendix A, for a detailed list of strategies.

As a board member on the planning team, you

- Ensure that as the planning team discusses lobbying strategies, all members understand and adhere to the legal guidelines for nonprofit lobbying.

- Tap your own history of involvement in advocacy work and share what you have learned about effective lobbying strategies and tactics.

- Observe, discuss, and expand your understanding of new strategies.

- Are innovative! Board members often know of other organizations and individuals who could be valuable partners in building a collaborative effort to move an issue forward.

---

[2] See also the material in Appendix B, page 84, on the legal limits of direct lobbying and grassroots lobbying.

Planning Step 6: Design organizational infrastructure

At this point in the planning process, the team has determined the value of advocacy and lobbying, proposed public policy goals, set criteria for selecting issues, identified issue priorities, and targeted arenas of influence. To actually engage in lobbying, the organization must have the internal capacity to carry out the work and to sustain it for the long term.

Decision making

One area of organizational capacity that needs attention is the establishment of decision-making structures: roles for the board, staff, public policy advisory committee, and a rapid response team. Clear lines of authority for decisions will enable the organization to function in a timely and effective way, even when it faces unanticipated crises or opportunities. See Worksheet 3: Decision Making, in Appendix A, for a list of decisions and a place to record who needs to be included.

Board members may play numerous roles in policy efforts:

- *The board:* The board has final authority over key decisions about policy work, including positions that the organization supports publicly. The board also makes major decisions about the allocation of resources to public policy work. And, in its governance role, the board is especially vigilant about ensuring that policy efforts do, indeed, further the organization's mission.

- *Public policy advisory committee:* Many nonprofit organizations form advisory groups, either as a committee of the board or as a panel of advisors that includes community stakeholders, to inform policy work. Such committees provide opportunities for airing ideas and assessing the pros and cons of various strategies, and often provide networking opportunities around policy initiatives. Interested board members often serve on such a committee and, when it is broadly expanded, serve as liaisons between the advisory committee and the decision-making board. Identify a policy committee structure that best suits your organization's unique style.

Policy Committee Gives Board a Policy Edge

Part of our work at the Council of Community Services of New York State (CCSNYS) is to ensure that the voice of New York's nonprofit community is heard in both local and federal political arenas. This directive was written into our strategic plan for ongoing development and investment of resources. To further this goal, CCSNYS initiated a Nonprofit Policy Cabinet that included several CCSNYS board members and a number of subsector agency representatives who could opt in or out of specific policy work depending on the issue at hand. Over time, we found the full Policy Cabinet becoming less and less active. In response, we modified our Nonprofit Services Committee to become our Nonprofit Service and Policy Committee. This committee is composed of fourteen board members, several of whom have been professionally engaged in the policy arena, and is staffed by senior CCSNYS management staff. The committee model allows CCSNYS to be more agile in our policy work, engage more board members in initial policy discussions, and move more quickly in forming recommendations. Rather than two or three board members having to coordinate with outside advisors and then go before their board peers to recommend policy agenda, we have several board members who are very active in our ongoing policy work and a full committee that makes overall agency recommendations on policy direction.

— *Denise Harlow, Director of Nonprofit Services, Council of Community Services of New York State*

• *The rapid response team:* Comprised of a few board members and key staff, this team is empowered to make decisions about fast-moving action in legislative arenas. Compromises, media opportunities, or ad hoc alliances may have to be addressed between board meetings, and this is the team to do it.

Staff roles

Board members support the executive director in efforts to determine staff responsibilities. Some specific staff roles may include the overall coordination of policy, direct lobbying, grassroots organizing, and media outreach. In the planning process, board members help to shape the staff's roles.

Staff and Board Members Make an Ideal Team

The Washington State Historical Society has a long-respected lobbying presence in the Washington State legislature. We have been successful on many budgeting issues. I think our success is due, in part, to the teamwork of the board and the executive director.

In anticipation of the upcoming bicentennial of the Lewis and Clark Expedition in the Pacific Northwest (2005–06), the Historical Society wanted to create an interpretive wayside project along a highway. To do so, we would need state funding so that part of a highway could be moved. The executive director of the Historical Society asked that I join him to meet with the senator who came from the county where the highway would be moved.

The director and I brought along a one-page sheet describing the project and what needed to be done, in layman terms, that we would leave with the senator. We spoke to the sena-

tor about why the project was important and, briefly, what sort of funding would be needed. The senator had asked the key staff person for the transportation committee to attend our meeting as well. Luckily our executive director had brought a more technical, two-page report about exactly what state highway funds would be needed for this project. This demonstrated to the senator that we were knowledgeable and had a well-thought-out plan.

I've learned that the executive director (or policy coordinator) has the day-to-day, on-the-ground experience, while board members have credibility in the community. Working together, the board member and executive director have the knowledge and influence needed to successfully make the case to an elected official.

— *Dave Edwards, Board President, Washington State Historical Society*

Resources

Board members help ascertain the financial resources and staff time needed to do advocacy work and also build and maintain the information and communication systems, internal and external, that allow the organization to be effective. The board's overall responsibilities for budgeting and fundraising extend to public policy work, and boards can be key to resource development. (Worksheet 4: Identify Resources, in Appendix A, provides a budget form for advocacy and activities.)

As a board member on the planning team, you

- Work with the planning team to clearly delineate board roles in public policy decision making. Everyone in the organization needs to clearly understand the board's responsibility and authority in making major policy decisions about advocacy and lobbying efforts and in approving budgets and fundraising strategies for meeting resource needs.

- Look at other organizations as models. If you have experience with other nonprofits' advocacy and lobbying, share that experience to help define roles, resources, and systems needs.

- Share your expertise about management information systems. Share what you know about maintaining databases of members, supporters, funders, and decision makers. Offer examples of good public policy web sites. Give staff feedback on proposed systems for tracking everything from meetings with legislators to media coverage of your nonprofit's advocacy efforts.

- Work to help shape realistic expectations for the costs incurred in policy work. Public policy work requires thoughtfulness, energy, creativity, and time. It doesn't always require much cash, but you do want adequate resources for staff and for information management and outreach systems that are essential to success.

Planning Step 7: Create the work plan

At this stage in the planning process, the team compiles all that it has considered:

- Mission, vision, goals
- Issues and arenas of influence
- Strategies
- Organizational infrastructure

Using Worksheet 5: Public Policy Work Plan, in Appendix A, or a similar format, the planning team drafts a comprehensive work plan proposal for the organization to review and for the board to debate, amend, and accept.

With any modifications mandated in the review process, the work plan becomes the document that guides the organization's public policy work.

Planning Step 8: Present the work plan

This is the final stage of the planning process. Staff and the board will review the planning team's proposal, and the board will take formal action to adopt the plan, perhaps with some recommended fine-tuning. Take the lead in acknowledging with other members of the planning team that you have made significant progress toward a focused and systematic approach to advocacy and lobbying for change:

- You have articulated your vision, goals, and policy objectives.

- You have taken the first steps in identifying the arenas of influence where your issues will be decided.

- You have chosen some general strategies for lobbying.

- You have planned the infrastructure that ensures your lobbying is an effective and sustainable strategy for fulfilling your mission.

What are the board members' roles in Steps 7 and 8?

- If you are a board member serving on the planning team, review the proposal carefully before it is deemed ready for full board review. Now that the plan is outlined in detail, are you convinced that it will lead to the desired outcomes? Is it true to your mission? Does it complement other components of the organization's program and service agenda?

- If you are a board member serving on the planning team, present the plan in the most interesting, thorough, and compelling way possible. Invite a thoughtful exploration of the vision, goals, policy positions, decision-making roles, and systems and resources required. Urge the organization's leaders to take time to understand and critique the plan so that everyone supports it. As one of the planners *and* a board leader, infuse your board colleagues with the same enthusiasm that you brought to the planning process!

- As a board member reviewing the plan (whether or not you are a part of the planning committee), be as involved with, critical of, and constructive about the plan for advocacy and lobbying as you would be in shaping the overall strategic plan for your organization. Ask questions. Probe to be certain that the plan addresses legal, governance, and resource issues adequately. Do a "gut check." Will this plan move your organization closer to meeting its mission? As proposed, will it make a positive difference for the people and places you serve?

- Be sure that you understand the expectations for board involvement in implementation of the proposed plan. Consider what you can contribute, as a board member and community leader, in the implementation phase.

- Take actions to amend the plan as needed. Once it is in a form that all agree advances your work, approve it and support it!

What can all board members do to support planning and implementation?

- Be prepared to volunteer for duties (beyond your role as a board member) that you are enthusiastic about tackling on behalf of your nonprofit's policy work.

- Prepare your list of contacts in the community who can add value to your nonprofit's policy work—as allies and advisors, as trainers and connectors.

- Be prepared to raise the funds for public policy work, implementing the fundraising strategies agreed to by the board once the planning team has presented their recommendations.

Once your organization adopts your public policy plan, advocacy and lobbying can become a high priority for meeting your mission. The next chapter examines specific lobbying and advocacy activities that board members most often undertake.

CHAPTER 3

Advocacy and Lobbying Activities for Nonprofit Boards

The importance of board members' involvement in planning has been underscored in Chapter 2. Important as it is, planning is only a means to an end: action on policy issues that advance your mission. At the action stage of advocacy and lobbying, board members as community leaders have extraordinary power and impact.

Why is it so important for board members to engage in their nonprofit's advocacy and lobbying efforts? You are positioned to be an effective voice for your organization's issues because of your stake in the organization and your standing in the community. Decision makers and policy makers understand that you serve on the board because you are convinced that the organization is doing something of value in the community. You volunteer time. You donate money to the organization. You shape organizational policy and direction. You have the best interests of the organization and the community served at heart. And you bear responsibility for the organization's integrity and accomplishment.

Volunteers who contribute to the organization, who represent the interests of the community within the organization's governance structure, and who work with the organization because they believe that its mission and programs are important speak with power in public policy dialogue. You speak to the issues from a selfless position and with a leadership role.

Who you are, your leadership in the community and your nonprofit, and what you know make you an important player in public policy arenas. And you are able to move your organization's agenda forward in ways that staff and other supporters cannot.

Lobbying: What Do Board Members Do?

Board roles in planning and governance have been discussed in the previous chapter—and should be nothing new, as planning and governance are key duties of the board. And in a general sense, board members are almost always advocates for their organization and its issues. Lobbying, however, is a new area for many board members. They and their organization's staff rarely maximize the potential of the board's strategic role in lobbying. To increase organizational presence and mission impact, board members can offer their time and talents in many ways:

• Board members provide access

• Board members use networks, build alliances, and help form coalitions

• Board members are powerful messengers in legislative arenas

Board Members' Voices Are Heard When Others Are Ignored

In December 2000, I joined the board of the Center for Human Development (CHD), an umbrella organization for over seventy-two human service providers in the Springfield, Massachusetts, area.

In spring 2001, board members of various human service organizations geared up to advocate for government funding to increase the salaries of low-paid human service workers. We wrote letters and e-mails and visited elected officials to request increased funding. Although unsuccessful, the board members continued to meet and set goals. In 2002, during the state's budget crisis, we rallied to prevent funding cuts to programs. Our goal was to create a new emphasis on administrative reform. In fact, we have had so much success with this effort, we've brought the salary issue back into the forefront.

I believe it has been extremely important that board members led these efforts because, in both cases, it wasn't our jobs on the line. We could speak from the point of view of a community leader, to tell officials what effect these issues have on our organizations *and* the communities we serve.

— *Bill Malloy, Board Member, Center for Human Development*

- Board members influence the executive branch of government
- Board members provide access

As a board member, you can expand your nonprofit organization's circle of influence. You know people in the community, in other nonprofit organizations, in philanthropy, and in arenas of influence with whom your organization's staff may not be as familiar. As a volunteer board member, you are in a strong position to provide introductions and help build relationships between your nonprofit's staff and the people you need as supporters for your organization's cause.

Advocacy and lobbying are components of nonprofit work that rely heavily on building strategic relationships for the present and the long term. You can support your nonprofit's effectiveness in building these relationships—with legislators, the press, funders, and community leaders. These strategic relationships with decision makers and opinion shapers are a crucial component of building advocacy and lobbying capacity.

Make phone calls to introduce your organization's goals to potential supporters. Arrange meetings between your nonprofit's staff and people who are key to your policy goals. Participate in those meetings and follow up with personal thank-yous to friends and colleagues who have been willing to open their doors (or checkbooks) to your nonprofit's staff and board.

Never underestimate the power that you have. Because of your position as a board member of a nonprofit, you can gain access to people with power. That is as true for the small, community-based nonprofit as it is for the larger organization. You can provide access to some elected officials simply because you are a constituent in their district. You

Think You've Got No Influence? Think Again!

Board members have real power, regardless of the size of their organization. Some boards attract people with long years of civic involvement, political connections, and clout. Other boards include people who are directly affected by the issues that the nonprofit addresses in its programs and services. Still other organizations attract people who have solid networks of people who can be tapped for donations, volunteer time, and grassroots lobbying efforts. Some board members serve because they are good idea people, strategists.

The size of a nonprofit organization is not the key determinant of board power. Power comes from the reality that you, the board member, have made a commitment of your ideas, energy, time, and money (even if only a small contribution) to an organization that you have determined is doing important work in your community. Your dedication, as a volunteer and as an organizational leader, gives you all the power you need to be taken seriously in arenas of influence. The title "Member of the Board of Directors" signals commitment, investment, status, and influence.

Make Certain Your Local Legislators Know Your First Name

There are many ways a board member can get involved in grassroots advocacy. As a member of the Minnesota Citizens for the Arts board, I have had the opportunity to spend a lot of time at the legislature, especially on our annual Arts Advocacy Days. I have testified before the Senate Finance Committee and have had the opportunity to sit in the house chambers and casually chat with representatives while they were taking breaks or having their lunch. I believe that none of these efforts would have been so effective if I was not on a first-name basis with my local legislators.

There was one occasion when Minnesota Citizens for the Arts had a statewide advocacy campaign for an important arts issue. Things were really heating up on a Saturday. I knew that one of our legislators always made a point of being available at the local café on Saturdays. We needed to know the position the house was taking on this issue. So, on a cold winter Saturday morning, I ran over to the café and had a very important and rewarding conversation with our local representation. Some of the best lobbying work can happen in your local café! It paves the way for equally important work at the state capitol.

It's important to remember that our senators and representatives are also our neighbors, our community members, and our representation in state government. They can help us get things done, and we can help them get things done. It's a partnership. Whenever I have an issue, I call or e-mail the senator and representative from my district, and their response is prompt, sometimes immediate, whether they're in Fergus Falls or Saint Paul.

— Rebecca Lynn Petersen, Board Chair, Minnesota Citizens for the Arts

can approach the press or donors, who will respond to you more willingly than to staff because you are a volunteer for your organization. You can connect your nonprofit to individuals in other organizations in which you participate—community groups, faith-based groups, labor unions, business associations, block clubs—and win new friends and allies for advancing your issues.

Board members strengthen alliances and coalitions

In addition to providing introductions and support for your organization's outreach to individuals, board members can build and strengthen institutional relationships. When your nonprofit has determined that outreach to another organization for the purpose of cooperating will build clout, you may be able to help as a liaison to the potential partner. If you have some affiliation and standing with the potential ally, so much the better. But even if you do not, participating in discussions that lead to a shared strategy for addressing the issue will enrich the impact of your nonprofit's effort. Board participation sends a clear signal that the board and organization are committed to building mutually beneficial alliances through networking, cooperation, collaboration, and coalitions. Your presence and your contributions to dialogue and negotiation may be the crucial factors in whether your nonprofit and a potential partner achieve a win-win agreement on behalf of shared policy goals.

Use Alliances for More Powerful Lobbying

In my experience, it has been easier to get attention for adequate funding than to achieve systemic changes. Getting laws changed is complex. Creating alliances within specific nonprofit groups (e.g., children, sexual assault, aging, domestic violence, mental health) can help organizations speak with a stronger voice and have a more definite influence in the political arena. Alliances can help your organization keep current on a policy issue, especially if each agency has a legislative/funding alert person to keep on top of developments (which sometimes change daily). Alliances can also help organizations hire professionals to craft proposed legislation, and paid lobbyists to map out strategies. After the plan is drawn up, it is important to include concerned individuals, community groups, faith-based organizations, elected officials, and human service agencies to create a team effort for achieving systematic changes. By collaborating, you have organized the power of many voices to move an issue forward.

— *Marvin Eckfeldt, President of the Board of Trustees, King County Sexual Assault Center*

Board members are powerful as key messengers

In every advocacy and lobbying effort, a critical calculation needs to be made about three points: key messages, audiences, and messengers.

What are our *key messages*? Key messages are the clear, brief statements about the problem, the proposed solution, and the rationale. They "make the case" for the policy change for which you are lobbying. Appendix C has information on how to shape key messages. See page 87.

Who are the *audiences* we need to reach? In any lobbying effort, there may be multiple audiences, including supporters, potential supporters, the general public, the media who reach target audiences, and ultimately the decision makers who have the authority to act on the issue.

Who are the *messengers* who can convey our messages to target audiences most effectively? Different messengers will have greater credence and appeal for different audiences. As a board member, you can speak with authority to the press on behalf of the organization. You can reach out to your organization's members and supporters as a spokesperson for the governance board and a voice for the organization's leaders. You can convey ideas and requests for action to decision makers with the power you have as a leader and as a person who cares about the issue from the perspective of the community's well-being.

There are three specific ways in which board members can serve as messengers: (1) participate in meetings with key audiences, including decision makers; (2) provide testimony on behalf of the organization in arenas of influence; and (3) write letters, make phone calls, and compose opinion pieces for newspapers.

1. Participate in meetings with key audiences, especially decision makers in legislative arenas: Board members who are also constituents of a targeted decision maker have a unique role to play, since elected officials and their staff are particularly committed to giving constituents opportunities to explain their issues and ask for a vote. But any board member who participates in a meeting with elected officials signals the organization's deep commitment to the cause and suggests that the community is watching the issue (and will hold decision makers accountable.)

Feeling Shy? Try on One of These Roles

In *Marketing Workbook for Nonprofit Organizations, Volume II*, Gary Stern describes four roles people can play to make things happen for their organizations. While Stern's advice is aimed at all kinds of marketing activities—from filling children's art classes to conducting capital campaigns—it applies equally well to the activities board members can undertake to gain access to legislators, executives, and other power brokers they wish to influence. The roles are ambassadors, door-openers, cultivators, and solicitors.

Ambassadors are scouts, identifying people who might be contacted and influenced. Even the shyest board member can play this role. Who on the board seems best at gathering information? There's your ambassador.

Door-openers are people who will lend their name and influence when making contacts, sign letters, make phone calls, and accompany solicitors on calls to smooth the way. Such a board member is likely well connected but may or may not be the outgoing type. Who on the board knows lots of people, grew up in the neighborhood, or clearly has connections? Congratulations, you've got a door-opener.

Cultivators make personal invitations, host events, and otherwise entertain the people you wish to get on your side. A cultivator may not be the most influential person but certainly loves to entertain, is gregarious, and is known for creating good feelings. Who brings homemade treats to each board meeting? Who buzzes about the room, making sure everyone is happy? Who is most likely to volunteer his or her home for the board retreat? Now you know who will be hosting any event where you wish to influence the influencers!

Solicitors are bold and willing to ask for commitment. Within the context of lobbying, the solicitor is ready to ask, directly, for what the nonprofit needs to better accomplish its mission. Who knows the facts and makes you want to join his or her side? Can anyone say salesperson? Now you know who you'll want for that final conversation with the mayor.

Your board probably has all four types, and a moment's thought will tell you who is best for what role. No doubt, if a type is missing, you can find the skill on your staff—and most people are capable of playing more than one role. The great thing about these roles is that everyone can play a part, and no one has to carry the full weight of your lobbying effort. Use each board member's native type to get your goals accomplished. And if you are the shy type, remember—it's about the mission. Keep your eyes on the prize and the rest will follow.

For more information on these roles, see the *Marketing Workbook for Nonprofit Organizations, Volume II: Develop the Plan*, by Gary Stern, available from the Amherst H. Wilder Foundation Publishing Center.

In addition, the experience and expertise that you have on your issue strengthens your nonprofit's position as a resource to the media and to decision makers and their staff. For example, staff of a nonprofit advocating for smoke-free public buildings invited a physician who serves on their board to meet with the Senate Health Committee chair. The physician provided compelling evidence to the chairperson about the health hazards of secondhand smoke. The committee chair then had the knowledge to make the case before the committee and invited the board member/physician to provide formal testimony before the committee to strengthen the case for smoke-free spaces.

Get the Most from a Meeting with a Legislator

Respect a legislator's time

More often than not, you will only get about fifteen minutes of lobby time with legislators. It is easy to talk on and on about something you are passionate about. Don't. You must keep your message brief. One time, I had only a few moments to get my message to a representative while she was running in the rain from one government building to the next.

Legislators hear from many lobbyists and have to sort through a lot of information. Always have a one-page paper with the message you want to leave with your representative. Make sure it simply states your key points and has contact information so the legislator can contact you with any questions.

It's a time for show and tell

Don't just tell legislators about your organization's need; tell them what you are doing to help yourselves. You need to be able to say, "Look, this is what we told you our priorities are, here's a graph that shows how we've been doing to help find money." When Washington did a statewide program audit, the Washington State Historical Society got very good marks. We made sure the legislators had access to this audit report. Try to demonstrate the quality of your organization's management. This will give representatives confidence that they are supporting a good thing.

Of course, it is important to explain your side of the story to a legislator. But you must also understand the whole issue. It is better to address up front any counterpoints your legislator might hear. You then have a chance to defend your stance and answer any questions the legislator might have.

2. Provide testimony on behalf of the organization in arenas of influence:
Board members are almost always treated with more respect than hired lobbyists (or even the organization's staff) in formal legislative proceedings. Your willingness to tell the personal story of why you are involved in the organization and the issue, your willingness to serve as a volunteer and dedicate your time to participate in the policy dialogue, and your standing as a member of the community all inspire respect for your participation. Your testimony matters.

Forge lasting relationships

Be respectful of new legislators. At the Historical Society, we make appointments with newly elected legislators, especially from the minority party, because they often have a little more time. We give these new legislators the same presentation we give everybody. You must remember that these elected officials will move up the ranks, and the partisan majority often switches.

When representatives are not in session, invite them to visit a program site. It is important that officials see what your organization does.

Be respectful of aides and secretaries. Legislators are busy people, and there have been times when I've had to leave my message with an aide. It is important to create a relationship with these people as well as with the legislator.

Find a mentor

As a board member, I think it is important to find a mentor who knows the ropes. A lot of what you learn about your political arena can only be learned through experience. Find someone who has met with elected officials in your area, and learn what has worked for them. I really had no interest in public policy until I became a board member and saw how the organizations I represented were affected by decisions that legislators made. In my case, it was an executive director of one of the organizations I chaired that had lobbying experience and was able to point me in the right direction.

— *Dave Edwards, Board President, Washington State Historical Society*

You may serve on your board because of your experience and expertise in the issue. For example, parents who serve on the board of a child care workers' organization can make a convincing case for livable wages for child care workers. Parents can tell real stories about the negative impact of high turnover in child care facilities and the negative impact of having highly trained and experienced professionals leave the child care field because of inadequate compensation.

Appendix C has more information on how to testify at a committee hearing. See page 88.

Testify—and Be Smart about It

I regularly advocate at city and county budget hearings on behalf of the Fremont Public Association, a $16-million multi-service agency that helps people living in poverty in the Seattle metro area. I've learned the following:

- Get there early. At a city council meeting there is usually a sign-in sheet. To have fresh listeners, you want to be one of the first four or five people to testify on an issue.

- Have the person from your organization most "in the know" about the issue type up talking points for you to have in your hand.

- There's a time limit. So try to get your point across quickly, but also add something personal. Use some facts, but also speak from the heart, from one person to another. Try to connect and you'll make your point more memorable.

For example, last year our mayor had proposed cutting funding for programs drastically. A coalition of human service groups in Washington State (including the Fremont Public Association) put a lot of pressure on the council, and later the council reduced significantly the number of cuts made by the mayor. This year, when testifying in front of the budget committee, I thanked them, saying something like "After what we went through last year, if I could give each of you a hug, I would." I was talking to each member of the committee as an individual person, and I hope it made my message (that funding our programs is important to the community) more memorable. This year the council did not cut the budget for human services.

— *Sarajane Siegfriedt, Board Member, Fremont Public Association*

3. Write letters, make phone calls, compose opinion pieces for newspapers: Calls, letters, and editorials are all tools of communication in a lobbying effort, especially when the issue is one with broad general interest. Your strategy is to build public awareness and support for the long-term work you do on your priority issues. Board members who make calls and write letters are believable advocates for their cause. Your status as constituent, community leader, and board volunteer serves in this instance, as elsewhere, to make yours an important voice. More advice on contacting legislators can be found in Appendix C on page 90.

Board members influence the executive branch of government

The executive, or administrative, branch of government plays a key role in shaping public policy. Governors, commissioners, and mayors can develop policy and funding proposals that shape priorities in all segments of community life. You, the board member, may already have or can easily build relationships with executive branch officials, agency directors, and staff within agencies. These connections will allow you to seed discussions with information and issues that need to be addressed.

Following are three approaches you can take to maintain good relationships with the people in the executive branch who have an impact on your mission: (1) work from the bottom up, (2) work from the top down, and (3) maintain systematic communications.

1. Work from the bottom up: More than one nonprofit issue has been saved from the veto pen by a governmental agency director who advised a governor to follow a legislative recommendation and keep a nonprofit's priority in place. Therefore, it makes sense to work from the bottom up to gain executive branch support and endorsement for your position and to insulate your issue against a veto.

Know which agencies have policy and funding authority in your issue areas. Learn about the organizational structure in those agencies that have policy and funding authority over your issues. Build ongoing strategic relationships with these agencies' program managers and leaders. These people make recommendations about your program. They can also alert you to anticipated opportunities or crises.

Build relationships with the people who control your funds. If you get government grants or contracts, be certain that the contract officers who administer your funding and monitor your work understand why you, a board member, value this support.

Become a trusted resource to administrative offices. Make it your goal as a board leader to be a resource to administrative departments and executive offices as they develop new policies and set priorities. If agency staff accept your ideas for how to solve problems, they are in a position to make recommendations to agency directors. When this happens, your ideas may turn into a governmental agency's recommendation to a mayor or governor. *Thus, you get a voice in the developmental phase of policy shaping and budget planning.* This is a plus for your nonprofit's lobbying campaign.

2. Work from the top down: Build upon existing relationships with the chief executive, or work to get to know this leader. As a board member, you may gain access more readily than staff. You will have a better chance of gaining the chief executive's support if you make sure he or she has had a chance to understand your cause and looks to you for reliable information.

Know the chief executive's priorities and positions on the issues that you care about. This information can be gathered from campaign statements, public statements while in office, and documents presented to the legislative branch and the public, including budget proposals and "State of the State," "State of the County," and "State of the City" addresses.

Know the responsibilities of the chief executive and the timeline for carrying out these responsibilities. Know when he or she presents budget proposals and annual reports to the legislature or other body, and what the rules are that govern veto authority and veto timelines.

Learn about the chief executive's staff and build on any relationships you have with people in key roles that affect your nonprofit's work. Positions that are usually most important are chief of staff, government relations director, and communications director (also called press secretary). Acquaint them with your organization and your public policy agenda.

Get to know the governmental relations staff person responsible for your issue area. He or she needs to know how you can be a resource in your areas of expertise. This is also the person who, along with the administrative agency director, will provide information to the chief executive to shape the executive branch agenda and make decisions about policies and funding that you propose. As a board member, invite the governmental relations staff to meet with you at your organization's location, if possible. Time your request for a meeting so that you have established this relationship before policy debates have begun and as the executive branch is shaping its proposals to the legislature.

3. Maintain systematic communications: Stay in touch with the executive branch. Call with new information or progress reports on your legislative initiatives. Alert executive staff to anticipated attacks on positions that you share with the executive branch.

As a board representative, thank the chief executive for any support. Awards, letters of appreciation, invitations to address your supporters at meetings or events, and letters to the editor applauding the chief executive's good work on your nonprofit's behalf will strengthen your relationship.

Other Roles for Board Members

There are key roles for you, a board member, in your nonprofit organization's public policy planning and direct lobbying. But you may also strengthen nonprofit advocacy efforts in many other ways, including the following:

- Serve on the policy advisory committee
- Serve on the rapid response team
- Support training and information gathering
- Help build and mobilize grassroots efforts
- Advocate through the media
- Raise money for advocacy
- Help build coalitions

Serve on the policy advisory committee

Policy advisory committees serve an organization well if they are created early in the development of public policy plans. For many organizations, the policy advisory committee includes board members and other stakeholders in the community. The committee members offer ideas, facilitate networking, evaluate plans, and often participate in advocacy and lobbying activities.

Roles for board members: Board members provide important support to advocacy work when they help to create a policy advisory committee, recruit other board members and community representatives to serve on the policy advisory committee, and participate in the committee's deliberations and activities.

Serve on the rapid response team

The board chair and at least one other board member need to be available for decisions about public policy initiatives when there is not adequate time for the full board or the policy advisory committee to convene.

Roles for board members: Offer to serve and agree to be available by phone or in person as needed, especially during peak periods of lobbying activity.

Support training and information gathering

Every organization can benefit from ongoing skill building and information gathering.

Roles for board members: Board members can urge their organization to invest time and resources in training for staff and supporters. Board members should invite skilled advocates, trainers, and policy issue experts to educate staff and supporters. You, the board member, do this to maximize opportunities for personal and professional development. When staff and board are *continuously gaining new skills and insights, the organization's capacity is expanded.*

Help build and mobilize grassroots efforts

Direct lobbying is only part of a nonprofit's lobbying strategy. To persuade elected officials to support your position, you will need grassroots support. Over the long term, your organization will need a base of supporters who will be citizen activists, contacting elected officials and the media in support of your goals. Calls, letters, and visits to elected officials and letters to the editor all influence elected officials.

Roles for board members: Identify individuals and organizations that are likely to care about your legislative issues, and introduce them to your organization's staff. As a community leader, you can help your organization identify stakeholders. (For a tool to help you analyze various stakeholder groups, see Appendix C, page 92.)

Advocate with others in your networks so that they "sign on" to your organization's advocacy and lobbying campaign.

Be willing to encourage board members of other organizations to use their community status as you are using yours: by being key messengers and reaching the media, the public, and elected officials.

If you have technical skills that will enhance your nonprofit's ability to communicate effectively with supporters—e.g., web site development, e-mail and fax alert systems—share your expertise.

Advocate through the media

Strategic media advocacy is an important extension of the strategic communications that you do when you lobby. Media coverage expands your ability to reach key audiences, including the general public, people who are affected by your issue, and elected officials and their staff.

Roles for board members: Share your media skills and contacts with staff who are building a media strategy. Be willing to be a spokesperson for your organization.

Raise money for advocacy

Your nonprofit's advocacy work plan includes a budget appropriate to the scale and scope of your advocacy effort. Most organizations do a small amount of lobbying without significant additional financial resources. But a major lobbying initiative and ongoing public policy capacity will require additional resources. Board members often work with staff to raise financial resources and request other donations from foundations, corporations, and individuals. Finding support for advocacy involves some unusual challenges. Private, corporate, and community foundations often think that they are not allowed to support advocacy and lobbying activity. Sometimes they know that such support can be legal, but they are not convinced that advocacy is worthy of charitable support. The sidebar Four Important Facts about Lobbying with Foundation Grant Funds, page 45, explains the rules.

Roles for board members: First, board members can make responsible decisions to allocate existing unrestricted funds and staff time to lobbying.

Second, once board members understand the rules that govern philanthropic giving for advocacy and lobbying, they can be effective in persuading foundation staff and trustees that this is a wise and appropriate investment that enables nonprofits to meet their mission. Board members can use their status to talk with reluctant funders about the advantages of supporting advocacy.

Third, local and national organizations, like the Alliance for Justice, Charity Lobbying in the Public Interest, Independent Sector, Council on Foundations, and others, sponsor briefings for funders. Board members can urge philanthropists to participate in such seminars. Increasing the awareness of the legality and benefits of funding advocacy can mean more funding for your nonprofit's issue campaigns.

Fourth, support your organization's efforts to raise resources for policy work in the same ways you support other development efforts: use your networks, friendships, and credibility in the community to identify potential donors; participate in meetings with funders; and urge others to support advocacy as an important component of nonprofit work.

Four Important Facts about Lobbying with Foundation Grant Funds

1. Public charities may use private foundation general purpose grant funds for lobbying.

   Charities are not disqualified from lobbying because they receive foundation funds, but charities and, even more, foundations have been slow to recognize and act on this fact. While grant funds from a private foundation to a charity must not be earmarked for lobbying, it is perfectly legal for the charity to use unearmarked general support foundation funds to lobby. Foundation funds are considered to be earmarked only if there has been an oral or written agreement that the grant will be used for specific purposes.

2. A private foundation is allowed to make a grant to a public charity to support a project that includes lobbying, but the grant must be used for the nonlobbying part of the project. The grant may not be earmarked for lobbying.

   A private foundation may make an undesignated grant to support a specific project that includes lobbying, as long as the grant is less than the nonlobbying parts of the project. For example, if a specific project has a $200,000 budget, of which $20,000 is to be spent on lobbying, the private foundation can give the project up to $180,000 because that part of the project budget is allocated to nonlobbying uses.

3. Community foundations may make grants to public charities that are earmarked for lobbying.

Community foundations are tax exempt under section 501(c)(3) of the Internal Revenue Code and are not treated as private foundations, so they are permitted the same lobbying latitude as public charities. For example, a community foundation that has elected to come under the 1976 Lobby Law may spend part of its annual expenditures on lobbying. It may also grant earmarked funds to a charity for lobbying up to the limits permitted by law. A community foundation grant, earmarked for lobbying, would count against the community foundation's own lobbying ceiling.

4. Foundations may fund a number of activities that are not considered lobbying under the 1976 Lobby Law but affect public policy.

   There are eight public policy–related activities that charities may conduct that are not considered lobbying under the 1976 Lobby Law and therefore can be fully funded by foundations. For example, a charity's response to written requests from a legislative body (not just a single legislator) for technical advice on pending legislation is not considered lobbying.

In short, there is considerably more latitude to use foundation funds to lobby than is commonly understood by many foundations and public charities.

Adapted from Charity Lobbying in the Public Interest web site, www.clpi.org.

Unique Coalition Rescues Utah's AmeriCorps

In July 2003, the Utah Commission on Volunteers, which administers the federal AmeriCorps* state funding for Utah, was informed by the Corporation for National and Community Service that due to a complex management and accounting error at the federal level, the Utah AmeriCorps program would be cut by 74 percent in the coming year.

It soon became clear that the only way to minimize the impact in our state was to encourage Utah's congressional delegation to enact legislation that would provide additional funding to support AmeriCorps.

This immediately highlighted a challenge to everyone involved in AmeriCorps. Federal AmeriCorps provisions expressly prohibit AmeriCorps members from "participating in efforts to influence legislation . . . or lobbying for [their] program; organizing a letter-writing campaign to Congress," and so on. How could we get involved in such an effort without actually organizing it?

This is where the Utah Nonprofits Association (UNA) stepped in and offered to serve as an intermediary to lead the effort to mobilize the Utah nonprofit sector in a grassroots effort to urge Congress to voice their opposition to the AmeriCorps cuts and to encourage Congress and the president to support the $100-million supplemental budget before them.

As part of their efforts, the Utah Nonprofits Association encouraged their nearly three hundred members and other partners via e-mail to call, write, and visit their U.S. representatives and to contact the White House. With information provided by the Utah Commission on Volunteers and local Utah AmeriCorps programs, UNA members wrote opinion pieces for local newspapers, arranged for media attention to the issue, and encouraged the general public to take similar action.

Several months later, we ended up with a cut of approximately 50 percent of the prior year's figures—half the funding and half the AmeriCorps members serving in Utah. While this is a significant cut that has had devastating results for communities in our state, we are grateful that it was not any more destructive, and that compared to other, nearby states, we did relatively well.

The partnership with UNA made a difference in our crisis, and I am grateful for the help and hope to continue to find innovative ways to work together in the future.

— *Scott G. Snow, Executive Director, Utah Commission on Volunteers–Office of the Lieutenant Governor*

Help build coalitions

In efforts to pass legislation on a policy issue, organizations may choose to work in collaboration with other organizations that share a common concern. Sometimes organizations willing to work in alliance have different but complementary strengths.

Roles for board members: Use your networks and knowledge of the community to identify potential partners and facilitate initial discussions about shared interests. Help staff determine whether a collaborative effort will further your cause. Ask questions: Do potential partners share a common objective? Do they agree on a shared lobbying strategy? Will combined efforts provide strengths that no group has alone? Do partners have the leadership and capacity to coordinate coalition efforts? Is each organization's unique contribution clearly understood?

Just a reminder: In all that you do to advance your nonprofit's advocacy and lobbying agendas, be sure that you are working as part of the team. As a board member, you have governance responsibilities for all aspects of the organization's activities. As a member of the policy team, you need to work with the staff and at their request. Coordination, consistency of message, and strategic action are the hallmarks of effective advocacy. Independent and uncoordinated actions can compromise or kill a fine plan, so teamwork and coordination are essential to maximize the board's value in policy work.

As part of the policy team, you, the board member, have a critical role to play. Advocacy and lobbying may be two of the most effective efforts you can make to advance your organization's mission—and now you know how to plan for and deliver a lobbying and advocacy agenda. In the final chapter you will find answers to some typical questions board members raise about advocacy.

CHAPTER 4

Frequently Asked Questions about Lobbying

Following is a list of questions often asked by board members interested in lobbying and advocacy efforts.

1. **Board members are responsible for the governance of a nonprofit organization. Why should I get involved in advocacy and lobbying?**

   Your governance role as a board member is your essential role in the organization. You shape the organization's direction, select and hold accountable its executive director, and ensure its fiscal health and compliance with legal requirements. In addition to these governance responsibilities, you have chosen to serve on the board to further the organization's mission and to contribute to the organization as a community representative, community leader, and volunteer. Advocacy and lobbying not only further your organization's mission but also help shape policies that better the community you represent. You have an important and powerful role to play in your nonprofit's advocacy and lobbying planning process. At the request of staff and the board chair, you can use your position in the community, your commitment to the organization, and your ideas to advance your organization's public policy agenda. Board members are effective in gaining access to elected and appointed officials, meeting with decision makers, providing testimony, writing letters, making calls, and more! Because you have standing in the community and have chosen to dedicate your time and talent to your nonprofit, you are a powerful spokesperson for its policy goals.

2. What constitutes lobbying, and how is it different from advocacy?

Advocacy involves embracing and promoting a cause in many ways. Lobbying is a specifically focused form of advocacy that is intended to influence legislation. Nonprofits lobby to pass laws that further the interests of the people they serve. They lobby to stop proposed laws that would have negative impacts on issues and communities.

3. What is the difference between direct lobbying and grassroots lobbying?

Direct lobbying is the action that you and your organization's members take to persuade elected and appointed officials to adopt your position and vote in a particular way on a specific bill. *Grassroots lobbying* involves educating, activating, and mobilizing supporters and the general public to influence decision makers to vote to support your positions. Both are important in nonprofit lobbying efforts.

4. Can 501(c)(3) nonprofits lobby? Is it legal?

Nonprofit 501(c)(3) organizations are not only allowed to lobby, *they are encouraged to do so.* Congress has made clear that nonprofits have a role in society that includes being a voice on the issues that relate to their mission. Nonprofits have great value to add to the public policy dialogue—information, expertise, and experience. And nonprofits are a vehicle for people who want to participate in the decisions that affect their lives. Lobbying is a great way for nonprofits to further their mission and involve members of the community in crucial public policy decisions.

5. Nonprofits have to report their lobbying, don't they? What is the "h" election that nonprofits can file to let the IRS know they want to be covered by specific reporting guidelines?

501(c)(3) nonprofits are allowed to do an "insubstantial" amount of lobbying, according to the tax code in the United States. Because this is such a vague standard, Congress passed the Tax Reform Act of 1976 and gave nonprofits an option of choosing a clearly defined set of limits for lobbying activity. Those guidelines are described in detail in Appendix B of this book. Nonprofits that wish to fall under the guidelines (and it is in their interest to do so) *must* file IRS Form 5768 (sometimes called the 501(h) election) to signal that they are following the lobbying guidelines known as the "lobbying-expenditures test." Many nonprofits choose the 501(h) election because it identifies clear measurements of how much lobbying you can do.

6. As a board member, am I allowed to contact elected officials on behalf of my organization?

Absolutely! It is, however, important to make those contacts as part of a strategic, staff-board plan. Board members and staff should shape their key messages and coordinate communications with decision makers and opinion shapers.

7. Are there model "job descriptions" for board members' roles in lobbying?

Thought you'd never ask! Here they are:

The board of directors: The board has final authority over the organization's policy agenda and the resources allocated to public policy work, consistent with the governance role of nonprofit boards. The board must ensure that policy efforts are helping the organization meet its mission.

The board chair: The board chair leads the board in ensuring that the organization has been intentional in adopting public policy as a component of its work. The board chair works with the board to affirm the organization's positions on public policy issues and to determine the priority of public policy in the overall mix of the organization's work. The board chair guides the board as it shapes plans and allocates resources for lobbying. In some organizations the board chair may be a community leader in a strong position to be a public spokesperson for your issue.

Board members: Board members make the key decisions to move the organization into public policy initiatives that are consistent with the organization's mission and goals. Board members may serve on the planning team that determines what role public policy will play in the organization's program, and they may also serve on the public policy advisory committee if one is created. Board members' responsibilities for the management of organizational resources and for organizational accountability are important in their governance of policy work. Often board members have relationships and status in the community that position them to be good spokespersons and lobbyists. Their role should include advocating on behalf of your organization's public policy positions in coordination with the board chair.

8. How does our board form and work with a public policy committee?

A public policy advisory committee can be either a committee of the board or an advisory committee that includes both board members and other interested stakeholders. This committee can add a focus and perspectives that an organization might not otherwise have. Its role can include shaping your organization's long-term policy agenda and assisting in building grassroots support for positions. A key role for this committee is to work with your organization in building strategic relationships with public officials, nonprofit colleagues, and other sectors.

9. How do board members get involved in responses to crises?

Nonprofits that lobby often create a rapid response team to address important issues that have to be decided quickly. The team includes the organization's executive director, one or more key board members, and the policy director or lobbyist. The team must be able to communicate quickly and make decisions during a fast-changing legislative process. Compromises, new ideas, media opportunities, and unexpected alliances will need to be addressed between regularly scheduled board meetings, and this is the team to do it.

10.   Who should decide on our nonprofit's lobbying agenda?

The planning process described in this book (and in greater detail in *The Lobbying and Advocacy Handbook for Nonprofit Organizations*) leads an organization through the process of shaping an issue agenda. Final decisions about issue priorities and basic positions, as well as resources allocated to lobbying activity, are the responsibility of the governance board. Board members usually make these decisions best when they rely upon recommendations from staff and members of a policy committee.

11.   What reports does my nonprofit have to make about our lobbying activity? Do I have to report my activity as a board member?

Nonprofits report their lobbying activity and expenditures on the IRS 990 filed each year. In addition, most states require nonprofits and all entities that lobby to report their expenditures for lobbying purposes. The office of the attorney general in your state can provide information about state-level reporting requirements. Nonprofit organizations that make the 501(h) election have to report direct expenditures for lobbying-related activities, staff time spent in preparation for lobbying (included related research), and payments to a contract lobbyist. Nonprofits that do not file the 501(h) election have to report all those activities plus the activities of volunteers. You and/or your organization should keep a record of your lobbying activity as a board member. If your organization has filed for the 501(h) election, your *time* is not reported to the IRS (since you are a volunteer your time does need to be reported as an expense), but it is useful to track anyway and may need to be reported at the state level. *Expenditures* that your organization makes related to your lobbying activity are reported to the IRS.

12.   Can 501(c)(3) organizations do educational work on issues in elections?

Nonprofits are encouraged to lobby but are prohibited from partisan activity. Election-cycle activities that are allowed include nonpartisan education on issues, reporting of voting records (but no scoring of candidates based on those records), candidate surveys with multiple and neutrally posed questions, candidate forums, voter registration drives, and get-out-the-vote efforts. Nonprofits may meet with candidates or parties to educate them on issues. In all activities, all candidates and parties must be treated equally. For specific guidelines and requirements for election-related activities, a detailed list of dos and don'ts, refer to publications by the Alliance for Justice (www.afj.org) and Charity Lobbying in the Public Interest (www.clpi.org). Note: Remember that while your activities on behalf of your nonprofit prohibit certain election-related actions, as a private citizen you have a wide range of election-related options—running for office, working on and contributing to campaigns, and more.

13. How can I learn more about the law-making process? Who are my legislators?

For state-level answers to these questions, go to your state legislature's web site. All states have such web sites. The best sites provide explanations of the process, names of committees and their members, and biographical information about legislators. Many states also provide a link to individual legislators' personal web sites. In addition to Internet-based information, most legislatures and local governments provide the public with written materials about members of the executive and legislative branches. The League of Women Voters in your area is a good resource for information about state and local elected officials. The secretary of state and the attorney general in your state will also have information about the law-making process and elected officials.

Some nonprofits help their staff, board, volunteers, and allies get to know the legislative process by inviting legislators and administrators to speak to their group and by conducting a "treasure hunt" at the capitol or city hall (see the sidebar on page 55).

In addition to your public policy–oriented tour, suggest that planning committee members take the architectural-historical tour of your capitol, often offered by the state historical society or capitol staff. These tours give historical context to the legislative process and provide some intriguing stories.

Treasure Hunt at the Capitol or City Hall

Directions: Plan a business-hours visit to your state capitol, county office, or city hall for members of your planning committee and any stakeholders you want to involve in your organization's lobbying effort. Allow three hours for this adventure. If possible, plan to visit with your own elected representative. Have fun on your "treasure hunt" as you do the following:

❑ Find the building. (Provide a map; one new lobbyist's first visit to her state capitol left her perplexed. There were no other cars in the parking lot. How could this be? She was at the nearby cathedral, which looks a lot like the capitol building but isn't!)

❑ Find the information office. Look for the house information office and the senate information office (except in Nebraska, which has a unicameral legislature).

❑ Collect all descriptive materials about the workings of the process.

❑ Get lists of elected officials, staff, committees, and rules.

❑ Meet the information office staff. Record staff hours and phone numbers.

❑ Ask what's on the web site.

❑ Sign up to get publications and meeting notices by mail or e-mail.

❑ Visit the index office. Ask how you get copies of bills, current calendars, agendas for legislative sessions, and official records of votes. Is there a system for tracking bills on the Internet? Ask for a demonstration of how to track a bill.

❑ Visit the legislative reference library. Is there one? What resources and services does it provide?

❑ Visit the legislative chambers. Where does the house, senate, county board, or city council meet? Ask how you get messages to elected representatives when they are on the floor debating issues.

❑ Visit committee meeting rooms. Where do the elected officials sit? Where do witnesses sit or stand when presenting testimony?

❑ Visit the press conference room. Is there a space for media events? How can you reserve it if you want to use it?

❑ Visit the press corps offices. Where are they? Stop and introduce yourselves.

❑ Where can people park? What are the public transportation routes for your constituents?

❑ Is the governmental complex fully accessible? Are there interpreter and translator services?

❑ Is there a cafeteria or other food service?

14. How do I get more information about lobbying Congress?

For information on the process, current activity on proposed legislation, and members of the U.S. House of Representatives and the U.S. Senate, visit Thomas Legislative Information on the Internet at http://thomas.loc.gov. An excellent resource, available in print or online at http://www.clpi.org, is Bob Smucker's *The Nonprofit Lobbying Guide,* second edition. This book is designed to guide nonprofits in lobbying at the federal level and includes valuable insights for state and local lobbying as well.

15. How can nonprofits get funding for lobbying? Can private or community foundations give grants to support lobbying activity?

It is useful to have undedicated funds—earned income, membership dues, general operating grants from private or community foundations—for lobbying. Community foundations are uniquely able and sometimes eager to support advocacy and sometimes lobbying. Work with your current funders and foundations that seem to share your goals to explore their interest in supporting your lobbying agenda. The Alliance for Justice provides training to grantmakers on the opportunities they have to support advocacy and lobbying. The Alliance for Justice publishes *Myth v. Fact: Foundation Support of Advocacy,* which includes detailed information about how much foundations can do to support advocacy (available at www.allianceforjustice.org). Charity Lobbying in the Public Interest has a letter from the IRS providing brief and clear guidelines for foundation funding of charities that lobby (available at www.clpi.org).

16. If we are part of a coalition, and our board and staff lobby on behalf of that coalition and not just our organization, do we report that as lobbying?

When you are representing your organization within a coalition, any lobbying that you do within that coalition counts as part of your organization's lobbying activities and expenditures.

17. Does lobbying that I do in my role as a private citizen count toward my nonprofit limit?

If you are not lobbying on behalf of your organization and in a coordinated effort for your organization's issues, your activity as a citizen *does not* count as lobbying for your organization and does not need to be reported to the IRS. Board members may do lobbying on behalf of several organizations in which they are active. Any lobbying you do for an organization counts for that organization's reports. If you act as a citizen lobbyist, your activity may need to be reported at the state or local level. Find out more by contacting the office of the attorney general in your state.

18. What is media advocacy, and when does it count as lobbying?

Media advocacy educates and influences the general public, opinion shapers, and decision makers and can be a powerful tool in a lobbying campaign. Media advocacy can take the form of radio, TV, and newspaper ads, news coverage of your issues, letters to the editor, and opinion editorials. Media advocacy includes both paid and earned media. These activities count as lobbying when they directly ask a decision maker to take action on pending legislation or when they ask others to contact decision makers about pending legislation.

19. Why lobby?

Because it may be one of the most effective strategies for meeting your mission and goals! Board members have power and influence, insight and experience that make a difference in a nonprofit's chance to lobby effectively.

20. Where can I get more information about nonprofit lobbying?

See Appendix D for a list of resources.

Afterword

You, a board member serving a nonprofit organization, have a critical role to play in making advocacy and lobbying effective strategies for meeting your organization's mission.

Your contributions are essential to your nonprofit's success in planning for public policy work, in shaping the policy agenda, in conveying key messages to target audiences, and in building broad support for your issues.

The best way to learn how much you can contribute to policy work is to engage in the process. Make advocacy and lobbying core to your active leadership for your nonprofit. As a board member, you have a unique position: volunteer, community representative, supporter, leader. You speak and act with a level of credibility that no one else enjoys.

Lobbying is honorable work. Nonprofit organizations dedicated to their mission and to enabling people to participate fully in a democratic society make a difference in how we care for one another. Your participation is key to nonprofit organizations' success.

APPENDIX A

Worksheets

Electronic versions of these worksheets may be downloaded off the publisher's web site. Use the following URL.

http://www.wilder.org/pubs/workshts/pubs_worksheets1.html?069393

These worksheets are intended for use in the same way as photocopies, but they are in a format that allows you to type in your responses and reformat the worksheets to fit your advocacy and lobbying effort. Please do not download the worksheets unless you or your organization has purchased this book.

There are two parts to this assessment. **Part A** *looks at the substance of your organization's public policy objectives.* **Part B** *looks at your organization's current capacity to do the work.*

Use this assessment to create a public policy readiness profile. This profile will show you how prepared you are to do this work effectively and examine your capacity to do the work. Refer to it as you complete planning and assess your first months of policy work. Mark your progress along the way. Remember that your response marks a starting point. Consider this a tool to inspire a sense of direction.

Part A: Public Policy Objectives

1. **What are your issues?**

   In the context of our mission, goals, and existing work, we have identified issues and objectives that can be furthered by engaging in debates about public policy and specific legislation.

   YES   NO   IN PROGRESS

   Our public policy issues are

2. **What are you already doing to address these issues?**

   We have organizational involvement and expertise in the public policy areas we most want to influence.

   YES   NO   DEVELOPING

   Expertise and experience are demonstrated in
   Programs:

   Services:

Research:

Education, awareness, community outreach:

Advocacy:

Lobbying:

3. **Where are your issues decided and debated?**

❑ Congress   ❑ City or County Agency

❑ State Legislature   ❑ Court

❑ County Board   ❑ Don't know

❑ City Council   ❑ Other: _____

❑ State Administrative Agency

Arenas of influence where we have an interest in shaping policy decisions are

4. **What policy changes do you want?**

We know the actions or changes that are needed in legislation to address the problems and opportunities that we have identified in our priority issue areas.

                YES   NO   SOME

Desired changes in laws, ordinances, or budget and tax policy are

5. **Will you be reactive or proactive?**

We will be proposing policy changes and need to prepare a campaign to introduce and lobby for a new idea.

       YES   NO

We will be responding to an existing legislative proposal or another group's efforts by supporting it.

       YES   NO

We will be lobbying to stop a measure that we think will have negative impact on our community or the people we serve.

       YES   NO

6. **Will you be lobbying one time only, or are you in it for the long haul?**

       ONE TIME ONLY   ONGOING COMPONENT

Check the approaches compatible with your organization's strengths and objectives:

❑ Background research and information gathering to "make the case"
❑ Public education and awareness
❑ Responding to issue alerts by organizations taking the lead on issues
❑ Direct lobbying of elected officials
❑ Mobilizing grassroots support
❑ Working with other organizations in a coalition or an informal alliance
❑ Media advocacy
❑ Other: _____

Part B: Organizational Capacity for Public Policy Work

1. **Who is the organizational champion of public policy work, and how deep is the organization's commitment?**

   The person(s) serving as key conveners of the discussions about policy work and the stewards of organizational readiness for policy work are

   Name: _____ Title: _____

   Name: _____ Title: _____

   Name: _____ Title: _____

   We have begun the organizational discussion about why and how to do policy work.

   YES   NO   IN THE SEEDING PHASE

   The board of directors has made a commitment to policy work.

   YES   NO   IN DISCUSSION

   Our organization's staff share a commitment to policy work.

   YES   NO   A FEW SKEPTICS

   Members, clients, stakeholders, and other supporters are ready to go.

   YES   NO   NEED TO TALK TO THEM

2. **Do you have a public policy plan?**

   Our organization is engaging in a planning process to decide how to incorporate public policy work into our organizational strategy and work plan.

   YES   NO   PLAN TO

3. **Who's doing what and when?**

   We have designated a person to coordinate our policy planning and work.

   YES   NO   RECRUITING

The role of the board is clearly defined.

      YES   NO   WORKING ON IT

Staff roles are clearly defined.

      YES   NO   WORKING ON IT

We have a "rapid response" team ready to make decisions and set the course for action when we are in the midst of fast-moving policy action.

      YES   NO   WORKING ON IT

We have decided to form an ongoing public policy advisory committee, and its role has been defined.

      YES   NO

4. **Where is the voice of the community?**

Community representatives shape our issue agenda. And we have systems in place to educate, inform, and mobilize our members and/or constituencies in support of our issues.

      YES   NO   WORKING ON IT

5. **Do you understand legislative processes and structures?**

We know how our state (or local) government moves an idea through the legislative process to become law.

      YES   NO   LEARNING

We know the key structures (house, assembly, commission, committee, political caucuses) and the players (leadership, members, staff) whom we will need to influence.

      YES   NO   LEARNING

6. **What are you prepared to do now?**

   We are ready to

   ❑ Compile and present the information that makes the case for our position
   ❑ Identify legislative proposals that affect our issues
   ❑ Identify decision makers and our supporters who are their constituents
   ❑ Monitor the introduction and progress of bills
   ❑ Record all of our action on our issues
   ❑ Inform all interested people as the debate progresses
   ❑ Issue calls to action to people ready to act
   ❑ Record all press coverage of our issue
   ❑ Maintain a record of our activity

7. **The best things are not always free. What resources will you commit to policy work?**

   We have budgeted for staff time, materials development, and information dissemination.

   | YES | NO | PLANNING FOR NEXT YEAR |

8. **Media matters. Are you camera ready?**

   We have included a media advocacy component in our lobbying plan.

   | YES | NO | WORKING ON IT |

9. **Nonprofits can and should lobby, but do you know the rules?**

   We understand the IRS rules governing 501(c)(3) lobbying and reporting.

   | YES | NO | WORKING ON IT |

   We understand the registration and reporting requirements our state has in place.

   | YES | NO | WORKING ON IT |

Read and discuss the following strategies. Select those that best fit your issues, objectives, and positions within the arenas you want to influence.

Direct lobbying strategies and tactics

Build positive relationships and trust with elected officials.
- ❏ Learn more about them, including their official responsibilities and policy priorities.
- ❏ Give them literature about your organization and policy objectives.
- ❏ Meet with them to tell them about your organization, programs and services, areas of expertise, and policy positions.
- ❏ Put them on your mailing list to receive news and updates.
- ❏ Invite them to your site to see your work and meet your supporters.
- ❏ Give awards to honor the work that they do.
- ❏ Other ideas:

Monitor the legislative process and identify activities that affect your issues.
- ❏ Read materials produced by the legislative body to track bill introductions and action on bills.
- ❏ Monitor Internet coverage of bill introductions, committee hearings, and committee and floor action.
- ❏ Have a person present in committee meetings to track the debate.
- ❏ Join existing coalitions or other organizations that are monitoring the issues that you care about.
- ❏ Monitor media coverage of legislative issues.
- ❏ Other ideas:

Provide expertise to elected officials.
- ❏ Help propose legislation. Verbally and in writing, present ideas for legislation to elected officials. Make the case for the idea. Include the desired changes in the existing or proposed law, the rationale for the change, and the desired outcomes.
- ❏ Provide reports and fact sheets that support the position you have taken on new legislation or on an existing proposal.

❑ Brief elected officials in person at their offices with information that you have.

❑ Be available to elected officials to provide expertise as the bill is developed and as they present their positions in committee meetings, caucus meetings, and floor debates.

❑ Conduct additional research as requested by elected officials.

❑ Identify nonprofit allies and work with them in efforts ranging from coordinated lobbying campaigns to formal coalitions to provide information on a shared priority.

❑ Research opposing viewpoints and be prepared to present the other side's view to elected officials so that they can anticipate the points that will be raised in a debate.

❑ Testify in legislative hearings as expert witnesses.

❑ Work with legislators throughout the legislative process to amend proposals and find compromise positions that are reasonable and further your cause.

❑ Other ideas:

Persuade legislators to support your position.

❑ Carry out a strategy that will gain media coverage of your issue and positive messages in support of your position.

❑ Write letters and make phone calls to key decision makers.

❑ Attend hearings and testify in support of your position.

❑ Involve people who are affected by the issue being debated; ask them to offer their stories and perspective in formal legislative testimony.

❑ Meet with legislators—first, committee members and leaders and, eventually, all members of the legislature—to persuade them to adopt your position based on the merits of the case and its importance to the people you serve.

❑ Other ideas:

Grassroots mobilizing strategies and tactics

Build your base of supporters.

❑ Identify constituencies that will be affected by decisions about your issues.

❑ Build lists of potential supporters, both individuals and organizations.

- ❑ Educate potential supporters about the issue through
  - ❑ Informational briefings
  - ❑ Newsletter articles
  - ❑ Special mailings
  - ❑ Individual conversations
  - ❑ Other:
- ❑ Invite potential supporters to sign on to your effort; as they do so, identify the actions they will take, such as making calls, writing letters, meeting with legislators, writing letters to the newspaper, testifying, and participating in rallies.
- ❑ Other ideas:

Mobilize your supporters.

- ❑ Create an ongoing flow of information and updates on the progress of your policy efforts through mailings, faxes, e-mails, newsletters, or web site postings. Include calls to action as appropriate.
- ❑ Maintain a system for asking supporters to act. Use phone calls, e-mails, faxes, and other alerts that explain which decision makers to contact, how to reach them, when to contact them, and what to say.
- ❑ Provide training for supporters in effective lobbying tactics.
- ❑ Create events that allow supporters to contact elected officials easily, such as "Day on the Hill" events or rallies.
- ❑ Ask supporters to allow reporters to interview them and use their experiences and concerns in media coverage of the issue.
- ❑ Other ideas:

Record below the individuals who have key responsibilities for decisions in your organization. This information will become essential in the fast-changing legislative environment. Keep it as part of your public policy guide.

Decisions to be made	Key decision makers
Adopt the organization's policy goals and strategies	
Shape the organization's policy agenda	
Set the organization's formal policy priorities	
Assign responsibilities to board	
Assign responsibilities to staff	
Allocate financial resources	
Manage organizational activity in carrying out public policy activities	
Approve public statements about the organization's position	
Approve positions in negotiations with elected officials when issues are in hurried stages of debate	
Other:	
Other:	
Other:	

Create a preliminary budget for your policy work. Determine the amount of time that each staff person will dedicate to public policy work and budget the required amount of salary and benefits. Plan for all related program activities, such as printing, postage, travel, and meetings. Don't forget administrative costs. Keep in mind that your organization may not have each of these policy positions. Determine who will have public policy responsibilities as a portion of the workload.

Item	Cost
Personnel: Salaries	
Executive director (% of time × salary)	
Public policy coordinator (% of time × salary)	
Lobbyist (% of time × salary, or contract fee)	
Support staff (% of time × salary)	
Other as determined by roles identified in your nonprofit	
Personnel: Benefits (% your nonprofit applies)	
Total Personnel Costs	
Public Policy Program Activities	
Technology: hardware and software, as determined by plans to reach elected officials and mobilize supporters	
Web site	
Broadcast fax	
E-mail	
Telephone	
Printing, as determined by plans for educational materials and alerts	
Postage	
Travel	
Board and public policy advisory committee travel to meetings	
Staff travel	
Public policy advisory committee meetings (space, food)	
Events (Day on the Hill, policy training, briefings)	
Administrative (% of organizational administrative budget as determined by % of overall work that is public policy)	
Other	
Total Program Costs	
TOTAL	

Use the following framework to draft a public policy work plan. Route the draft to the rest of the planning team, rewrite as necessary, and then seek the team's approval to send the plan to the board for approval. Save this as part of your public policy guide.

I. Organizational mission

II. Public policy vision and goals

A. Vision

In three years, as a result of our public policy efforts:

B. Goals

We have the following public policy goals:

III. Issues

For each issue, state the objective, the arena of influence where that issue can be addressed, and how the organization will lobby. Identify the roles and responsibilities of staff, the board, and volunteers in carrying out those lobbying activities.

Many organizations choose a single issue for their primary focus. Often this is the best approach, especially for an organization just beginning its policy efforts. In your plan, focus on just the one issue that will dominate your work in the next year. If you plan to address multiple issues, indicate which ones will get the emphasis in your work and which you might simply monitor.

Issue 1

Objective:

Arenas of influence:

Issue 1 work schedule:

Tasks/Activities	Who	By when

Issue 2

Objective:

Arenas of influence:

Issue 2 work schedule:

Tasks/Activities	Who	By when

Issue 3

Objective:

Arenas of influence:

Issue 3 work schedule:

Tasks/Activities	Who	By when

IV. Organizational infrastructure

A. Roles and responsibilities

Identify the positions and people required to deliver on the goals of the plan.

B. Decision-making authority

Insert and edit your completed Worksheet 3: Decision Making. (An organizational chart for your public policy work could be included here to illustrate the roles and responsibilities of the people involved and the lines of decision-making authority.)

C. Resources needed

Insert and edit your completed Worksheet 4: Identify Resources.

V. Conclusion

The 1976 Lobby Law

The 1976 Lobby Law established clear guidelines that nonprofits can choose to apply to their lobbying efforts. To be covered by those guidelines, your nonprofit must do a onetime filing of IRS Form 5768. If you don't file this form, your work will be judged on whether or not you do only an "insubstantial" amount of lobbying. This is a vague guideline that leaves nonprofits with uncertainty about how much lobbying is allowed. Therefore, most nonprofits should elect to fall under the clear expenditure test, a "bright line test" that allows you to track your lobbying expenditures and always know with great certainty that you are working within the guidelines of the law.

There are basic but important steps that your nonprofit should take to be certain that you are covered by the IRS 1976 lobbying expenditure guidelines.

1. Take formal steps to elect to fall under the 1976 guidelines

To elect to be covered by the rules, your organization must file IRS Form 5768 with the IRS. This is sometimes called the "(h) form" because it refers to Section 501(h) of the Internal Revenue Code. Your nonprofit needs to file this very simple one-page form just once with the IRS, at any time, and then your nonprofit will fall under the guidelines for as long as you choose. The IRS has provided clear documentation to nonprofit organizations that filing this form is favored by the IRS and will not trigger an audit or any other activity that should concern you. Organizations that elect to fall under the rules have an easy way to account for their lobbying expenditures and provide clear information to the IRS. Everyone appreciates clarity on this issue.

2. Know the lobbying limits

The 1976 Tax Reform Act divides lobbying into direct lobbying and grass-roots lobbying.

Direct lobbying occurs when an organization communicates its position with regard to legislation or legislative proposals directly to legislators, legislative staff, executive branch officials, and executive staff.

Grassroots lobbying occurs when an organization asks the public to support, oppose, or otherwise influence legislation by contacting elected and appointed officials. A grassroots lobbying effort is most frequently identified by a "call-to-action" phrase such as "call your congressperson today to ask them to vote YES on HF 123." Call-to-action phrases are commonly used in action alerts and press releases.

Figure 1 shows the guidelines for lobbying expenditures.

Figure 1. Lobbying Limits under the Expenditure Test

Exempt Purpose Expenditures*	Total Lobbying	Grassroots Lobbying
Up to $500,000	20%	5%
$500,000 to $1,000,000	$100,000 + 15% of excess over $500,000	$25,000 + 3.75% of excess over $500,000
$1 million to $1.5 million	$175,000 + 10% of excess over $1 million	$43,750 + 2.5% of excess over $1 million
$1.5 million to $17 million	$225,000 + 5% of excess over $1.5 million	$56,250 + 1.25% of excess over $1.5 million
Over $17 million	$1 million	$250,000

* In reviewing this chart, note that your organization's "exempt purpose expenditures" are all payments that you make in a year except investment management, unrelated businesses, and certain fundraising costs. "Certain fundraising costs" includes the cost of external fundraising consultants, an in-house fundraising department of two or more people who spend the majority of their time on fundraising, or any separate accounting unit that is designed as a fundraising department. (See IRS regulations for a full description of excluded expenditures.)

Figure 1 clearly shows that nonprofits that elect to fall under the guidelines may comfortably expend a significant amount on lobbying, with more spending allowed on direct lobbying than on grassroots lobbying. For example, an organization that made exempt expenditures of $1.2 million could spend up to $195,000 on *all* lobbying ($175,000 plus 10 percent of $200,000). Of that $195,000, a maximum of $48,750 could be spent on grassroots lobbying ($43,750 plus 2.5 percent of $200,000).

Why your organization should elect to fall under the 1976 Lobby Law

If you choose to fall under the expenditure test . . .

If you elect to fall under the expenditure test and file IRS Form 5768, clear guidelines govern what you can expend on lobbying. There are three benefits to falling under the guidelines.

1. The penalties for exceeding the lobbying expenditure limits are much less severe than the failure to meet the insubstantial-lobbying test. Violations of the expenditure limits usually result in tax penalties, and a nonprofit would only lose its tax-exempt status under extraordinary circumstances.

2. Lobbying is measured by expenditures. This sets clear, specific, measurable guidelines for lobbying.

3. There are specific definitions of what activities related to legislation do not count as lobbying. For nonprofits that elect coverage under the 1976 Lobby Law, activities that do not count toward lobbying limits include

   • Contacts with elected officials or executive branch representatives about proposed regulations (as opposed to legislation).

   • Lobbying by volunteers. (No monetary value is assigned to the time volunteered.)

   • Communication with the organization's members on legislation as long as there is no call to action.

- A nonprofit's response to written requests from a legislative body for technical advice on pending legislation.
- Self-defense lobbying, such as lobbying on issues that affect the organization's existence relative to tax status, powers, or lobbying rights. (Lobbying for program funding *does* count as lobbying; lobbying to protect your right to lobby does not.)
- Disseminating the results of nonprofit research and analysis if presented in a fair and full way so that the audience could form an independent opinion.

If you choose not to fall under the law . . .

If you take no action, your organization will be covered by the vague IRS assessment of whether your organization does any substantial lobbying. Cases are decided on an individual basis and leave nonprofits struggling with uncertainty. Under the insubstantial-lobbying test the penalties for what the IRS determines is "substantial" are quite severe. Under this test, a nonprofit can lose tax-exempt status and the right to receive tax-exempt charitable donations.

Clearly, it is in your nonprofit's best interest to elect to fall under the 1976 Lobbying Law and to file the proper paperwork immediately.

Lobbying Tips

Shape Key Messages as You Write Your Proposal

Your organization needs to shape its key messages in the early stages of preparing your legislative work. *Key messages* are clear and consistent statements about the issues, ideas, and actions that you are promoting. They are a critical part of the way you build understanding and motivate people to respond. Your organization will need to identify the key messages that you want to convey, the audiences that you are targeting, and the vehicles that will help you to get your key messages to your target audiences. In lobbying, key messages usually include the following:

Case statement: This is a clear articulation of the problem that you have identified, the solution and position that you are advocating, and the rationale that supports your position.

Results: You need to state the expected outcomes of your proposed solution to a problem and identify the ways in which those outcomes will be measured and experienced. Be as clear as possible in describing how people's lives and communities will be different if the measure you support passes or the measure you oppose is allowed to progress. For example, advocates of clean and safe water policies need to address the specific consequences of allowing fertilizers and manure to run into streams, rivers, lakes, and aquifers as part of a campaign to stop feedlots from expanding.

Slogans: Your lobbying campaign will want to include repetition of key phrases that capture the essence of the issue. For example, advocates for violence prevention have repeated one brief slogan as part of every written statement or public notice, whether it is about stopping domestic abuse or ending gang warfare: "You're the one who can make a difference. You can make the peace."

Persuasive statements: These are the often-repeated statements that capture your ideas and touch the particular audience that you have targeted. These statements appeal to a specific audience's interest in the issue. Advocates for the right to bear arms have approached mothers with the statement, "You not only have a right to protect your children, you have a responsibility." They might reach another targeted audience, hunters, by noting that "It is part of the American way of life. Don't let anyone limit your right to hunt." To yet another target audience, lawmakers, they might use persuasive statements relying on legal issues and election strategies: "The Constitution guarantees the right to bear arms. Voters in your district—lots of hunters—want to be able to hunt and protect their property."

Marketing techniques can have great application to this aspect of lobbying. For in-depth study of nonprofit marketing, including strategies for targeting audiences and shaping key messages, see Gary Stern's *Marketing Workbook for Nonprofit Organizations Volume II: Mobilize People for Marketing Success.* Publication details are included in Appendix D.

How to Testify at a Committee Hearing

Committee testimony is one form of formal, strategic communication. Your lobbyist and the bill's sponsors can help you arrange to testify. You have already prepared your key messages as you developed your lobbying materials. Draw your testimony from your key messages. (See the preceding section Shape Key Messages as You Write Your Proposal in this appendix.) Make your testimony clear, brief, and compelling. Use real-life stories to make complex issues meaningful and personal. Following are some tips for testifying.

Prepare a formal statement of your position. Explain your position in clearly enumerated points. This can range from a one-page handout that is the most direct statement of your position to letters of support, press clippings, pictures, and artifacts.

Learn everything possible about the committee members. It is important to know the audience. And legislators are always pleased to be addressed by name.

Choose a person to provide your primary testimony. Choose someone who is articulate and convincing and has status within your organization or coalition. Your board chair, executive director, or the staff person with the highest level of expertise may be more appropriate for this role than your lobbyist, who serves as "stage manager." The organization needs its best and most influential voice.

Provide an additional person or two to testify. Choose people who can state why they support your position and how they expect it to impact their lives or communities. If time is limited, include their stories in written form.

Respect committee protocols. Address the committee correctly (Madam or Mister Chair and Members of the Committee). Respect time constraints.

Anticipate questions and opposition. Research who opposes your position, why, and what they are saying about the issue. Assume that opponents, too, will have lobbied committee members and their staff. Assume that you will get requests to explain your facts. Also be prepared for questions driven by a different position or perspective on the issue. You and your legislative supporters should identify these potential questions and how you will address them. Write out the questions and answers to the best of your ability.

Rehearse, critique, revise.

Relax. Remember that you know more about your issue than almost anyone else in the process, and you are prepared to make a case for something that matters. Square your shoulders, take a deep breath, and do your best.

Ask the committee members to vote in support of your position.

Tips and Tactics for Contacting Legislators

Meeting with legislators

Make an appointment to see your legislator. If you have not set up an appointment, you may still be able to meet with your elected officials. Stop at your legislators' offices, and ask their staff if the legislator has a few minutes to meet with you. Even on busy days, many legislators will make time for a conversation with a constituent, so be sure to tell staff and legislators that you live in the district.

For a short but effective discussion:

1. Introduce yourself. Note if you are a constituent. Thank the legislator for taking the time to meet with you. Identify your organization if you are working for a nonprofit or coalition. Tell a little about your mission and the people served (keep it brief).

2. State your purpose. Be clear about what legislation you are supporting or opposing. Mention it by bill number and topic. Focus on one topic per meeting. Let the legislator know your position and why you are asking him or her to vote for that position.

3. Let the legislator and his or her staff members know that you and your organization have information and expertise. Let them know you can be a resource for them.

4. Give the legislator a chance to talk about his or her perspective on your issue.

5. Ask for the legislator's vote, and try to get a commitment at the meeting. If the legislator is reluctant to commit, ask what information would be helpful, and provide it.

6. Let them know you plan to stay in touch.

Keep it brief. Expect to have five- to ten-minute conversations if it is a busy time in the legislative session. Follow-up will enhance this brief meeting, so write a follow-up letter as soon as possible.

Making phone calls

1. State your name, address, and organization, and indicate that you are a constituent if that is the case.

2. Give the name and house or senate file number of the legislation, or clearly explain the issue.

3. State whether you oppose or support the legislation, and how you want your legislator to vote. Include a statement on how the issue affects you personally.

4. You will usually be speaking with a secretary or an aide who is checking pro or con, and the call will last a very short time. Keep the phone call under five minutes unless the aide or legislator prolongs the conversation.

5. Listen to the legislator's point of view.

6. Take down the name of the aide with whom you spoke so that you will have a contact person in case you need to contact the legislator again.

7. Thank them for their time, both on the telephone and with a note of thanks for the conversation that includes a concise summary of your opinion.

8. Do not call too often and risk becoming a nuisance.

9. Do not lie or try to talk your way around questions to which you do not know the answers. Say that you will get back to the legislator or aide, and then do so.

Writing letters

1. Use the correct address and salutation (e.g., Dear Senator *name*, or Dear Representative *name*, or Dear Governor *name*). While the legislature is in session, send letters to senate or house offices.

2. Describe the bill by popular name and by house or senate file number, or clearly describe the issue.

3. Be brief and clear. Write about one issue per letter, and state the issue and how you want your elected official to vote in your first sentence. Letters should be no longer than one page; however, longer letters may be appreciated if you have some new information about the subject.

4. Be specific. If possible, give an example of how the issue affects your district.

5. Be timely. Make sure your legislator will have sufficient time to consider your request.

6. Know your facts. Inaccurate or misleading information will hurt your credibility.

7. Be polite in your requests for support or opposition. Never express anger, make demands, or threaten defeat at the next election. You will want to have future contact with the legislator.

8. Use your own words and stationary rather than form letters or postcards. In addition, write legibly or type—your letter could be discarded if it is not easy to read.

9. Be constructive. Explain an alternative or better solution to the problem, and offer to be a resource for the issue.

10. Send a note of appreciation when your elected official supports your issue. When he or she does not support your issue, explain why you think a different decision should have been made. It might make a difference the next time.

How to Conduct a Stakeholder Analysis

Stakeholders are all the people who have an interest in your organization's success at achieving its mission. In public policy work, stakeholders include the people who care about your effectiveness in passing or stopping legislative proposals. In a stakeholder analysis, you identify the specific segments of the general public who care about your organization's work and public policy agenda. For each of your public policy goals, you may have different stakeholders.

Begin your analysis by stating your organization's mission and one public policy goal that you will advance to meet your mission. Then brainstorm to construct a list of all the people or groups that might be affected by or care about this goal. These stakeholders will include the following people and groups.

People and groups that will benefit from the proposed law. These may include your constituents or members, other people who struggle with the problem you are attempting to solve, groups and individuals who support the intended beneficiaries of the proposed law, and people in other states or countries who will base their efforts to change laws on the precedents that you set. You need to get these stakeholders involved in your effort so they can tell their own stories, persuade decision makers that the problem you have named is real, and emphasize that the proposed solution will help.

People and groups that will benefit from your organization's success. These stakeholders include board, staff, donors, and funders who support your work; allied organizations that rely on your services; and similar organizations that want to follow your model. This group of stakeholders is likely to rally behind you because they are loyal. You will need them to use their power as constituents, experts, and informed citizens to help make your case to decision makers.

People and groups that influence opinion and make decisions. These stakeholders include the people whose support you need in order to convince elected officials to adopt your position: community leaders, political leaders, and members of the media; the elected officials who will vote on your proposal; and the executive branch leaders who will support, oppose, or veto your proposal. These opinion influencers and decision makers are the ultimate targets of your efforts because they shape the policy dialogue and make policy decisions.

For each group of stakeholders, you will need to determine

1. Which issue they care about
2. Why they care
3. What they can do
4. What you want them to do
5. How to present your key messages so that you persuade them to join your cause
6. How you will reach them, educate them, and keep them up-to-date on your issues and arguments
7. How you will mobilize them to act strategically at critical times

After you have determined your stakeholders and the kinds of activities necessary to educate and motivate them, you will need to set priorities; rarely will you have enough resources or time to reach *all* your stakeholders. Placing your stakeholders on an x-y grid such as the one below can help you decide which ones you had best concentrate your energies on. Rank them by influence (on the vertical axis) and ease of accessibility (on the horizontal access). Concentrate your actions toward the upper left of the grid—but don't forget that many voices with "low influence" can become *very* influential when combined.

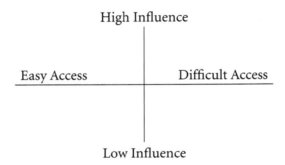

Decide which stakeholder groups are priorities based on how much they can influence the people who will be making decisions about your legislative proposals. Focus your time, energy, and resources on these stakeholders. Build your efforts to educate and mobilize supporters around the insights gained from this stakeholder analysis.

APPENDIX D

Resources

Publications

Essential reading for nonprofit lobbying

Amidei, Nancy. *So You Want to Make a Difference: Advocacy Is the Key*. Washington, DC: OMB Watch, 1999.

> This guide for individuals and organizations explains the many dimensions of advocacy and provides useful tips on how to make a difference. It includes basic information about how government is structured and how the legislative process works, especially at the national level. Amidei includes many stories of how individuals have been effective advocates.

Avner, Marcia. *The Lobbying and Advocacy Handbook for Nonprofit Organizations*. Saint Paul, MN: Amherst H. Wilder Foundation, 2001.

> *The Lobbying and Advocacy Handbook for Nonprofit Organizations* is the source and companion book for this text, aimed at boards. It contains indepth instructions for all of the processes described in this text, plus much more. It is more than most board of directors need, but those board members on the planning committee will need the complete text.

Center for Community Change. *How and Why to Influence Public Policy: An Action Guide for Community Organizations*. Washington, DC: Center for Community Change, Issue 17, Winter 1996.

> This is an easy-to-read, excellent resource on grassroots lobbying and specific strategies for building persuasive issue campaigns.

Cohen, David, Rosa de la Vega, and Gabrielle Watson. *Advocacy for Social Justice: A Global Action and Reflection Guide.* Bloomfield, CT: Kumarian Press, 2001.

This guide for social justice is intended for the practitioner, trainer, and student of activism. It includes a tool kit for taking action and has a companion web site with updated information on organizations and resources. It includes case stories focused on international advocacy initiatives.

Harmon, Gail M., Jessica A. Ladd, and Eleanor Evans. *Being a Player: A Guide to the IRS Lobbying Regulations for Advocacy Charities.* Washington, DC: Alliance for Justice, 1995.

This guide provides clear and detailed information about IRS regulations regarding lobbying activities by public charities. Topics include basic law on lobbying activity, definitions of lobbying, ways to determine lobbying expenditure limits, and forms for tracking and reporting lobbying activity.

Kingsley, Elizabeth, Gail Harmon, John Pomeranz, and Kay Guinane. *E-Advocacy for Nonprofits: The Law of Lobbying and Election-Related Activity on the Net.* Washington, DC: Alliance for Justice, 2000.

E-Advocacy covers Internet tools, lobbying law, and election-related advocacy law. This is an excellent guide to how nonprofits can use the Internet for lobbying and electoral advocacy within the law. It is available at the Alliance for Justice web site, www.afj.org.

Smucker, Bob. *The Nonprofit Lobbying Guide,* 2nd ed. Washington, DC: Independent Sector, 1999.

This is a comprehensive guide offering inspiring discussion of the reasons for nonprofits to lobby, detailed how-to lobbying information focusing on national legislation, technical information about nonprofit lobbying and the law, and statements (and stories) from notable leaders in the nonprofit sector about lobbying. The entire text is available online from Charity Lobbying in the Public Interest at www.clpi.org.

Other helpful reading

Asher, Thomas R. *Myth v. Fact: Foundation Support of Advocacy.* Washington, DC: Alliance for Justice, 1995.

Barry, Bryan W. *Strategic Planning Workbook for Nonprofit Organizations, Revised and Updated.* Saint Paul: Amherst H. Wilder Foundation, 1997.

Berry, Jeffrey M., with David F. Aarons. *A Voice for Nonprofits.* Washington, DC: Brookings Institution Press, 2003.

Bryson, John. *Strategic Planning for Public and Nonprofit Organizations.* San Francisco: Jossey-Bass, 1988.

Colvin, Gregory L., and Lowell Finley. *Seize the Initiative.* Washington, DC: Alliance for Justice, 1996.

Minnesota Citizens for the Arts. *Arts Advocacy Handbook.* Minneapolis: Minnesota Citizens for the Arts, 1997.

O'Connell, Brian. *People Power: Service, Advocacy, Empowerment.* New York: Foundation Center, 1994.

Reid, Elizabeth J. "Nonprofit Advocacy and Political Participation" in *Nonprofits and Government: Collaboration and Conflict,* ed. Elizabeth T. Boris and C. Eugene Steuerle. Washington, DC: Urban Institute Press, 1999.

Sparks, John D. *Lobbying, Advocacy, and Nonprofit Boards.* Washington, DC: National Center for Nonprofit Boards, 1997.

———. *Best Defense: A Guide for Orchestra Advocates.* New York: American Symphony Orchestra League, 1995.

Stern, Gary. *Marketing Workbook for Nonprofit Organizations Volume I: Develop the Plan.* 2nd ed. Saint Paul: Amherst H. Wilder Foundation, 2001.

———. *Marketing Workbook for Nonprofit Organizations Volume II: Mobilize People for Marketing Success.* Saint Paul: Amherst H. Wilder Foundation, 1997.

Worry-Free Lobbying for Nonprofits: How to Use the 501(c)(3) Election to Maximize Effectiveness. Washington, DC: Alliance for Justice, 1999.

Organizations

Information and training on nonprofit lobbying

Advocacy Institute
1629 K Street NW, #200
Washington, DC 20006
Phone: 202-777-7575
Fax: 202-777-7577
Web site: www.advocacy.org

The Advocacy Institute is a U.S.-based global organization dedicated to strengthening the capacity of political, social, and economic justice advocates to influence and change public policy.

Alliance for Justice
11 Dupont Circle NW, 2nd Floor
Washington, DC 20036
Phone: 202-822-6070
Fax: 202-822-6068
Web site: www.afj.org

The Alliance for Justice offers detailed information online and through a wide variety of publications and training events on nonprofit political activity with an emphasis on laws that govern nonprofit lobbying and activity in election cycles.

Charity Lobbying in the Public Interest
2040 S Street NW
Washington, DC 20009
Phone: 202-387-5048
Fax: 202-387-5149
Web site: www.clpi.org

Charity Lobbying in the Public Interest provides guidelines specific to nonprofits on why and how to lobby, materials on laws that govern nonprofit lobbying, a list of nonprofit lobbying resource people in more than eighteen states, written and audiovisual training materials, training guides and curricula, training, and support.

Independent Sector
1200 Eighteenth Street NW, Suite 200
Washington, DC 20036
Phone: 202-467-6100
Fax: 202-467-6101
Web site: www.independentsector.org

Independent Sector is an association of charitable, educational, religious, health, and social welfare organizations. Contact the association for information about issues affecting the nonprofit sector and information resources.

National Council of Nonprofit Associations (NCNA)
1030 Fifteenth Street NW, Suite 870
Washington, DC 20005
Phone: 202-962-0322
Fax: 202-962-0321
Web site: www.ncna.org

Contact NCNA to find out if your state has an association of nonprofits and how you can access information and training.

OMB Watch
1742 Connecticut Avenue NW
Washington, DC 20009-1171
Phone: 202-234-8494
Fax: 202-234-8584
Web site: www.ombwatch.org

OMB Watch focuses on a number of issues important to nonprofit organizations, including federal budget and government performance issues, regulatory and government accountability, information for democracy and community, nonprofit advocacy, and nonprofit policy and technology. Contact OMB Watch for information on any of these topics, including advocacy.

Information about state and local legislative arenas

As you seek information about state and local legislative bodies, their web sites will be an excellent starting point. All states, most counties, and many cities have their own home pages. These often link you to vital information about the community, the form of government, the names and contact information for appointed and elected officials, descriptions of information resources and services, details about the policy-shaping process and opportunities for public input, and calendars of meetings and agendas.

Key sites are identified here that will lead you to general information about state and local government and links to the web sites for your own city, county, and state.

The National Association of Counties

The National Association of Counties provides this site that allows you to select the state in which you are interested and call up links to all the counties within that state with web sites. www.naco.org/counties/counties/index.cfm

The National Council of State Legislatures

The National Council of State Legislatures site, NCSLNet, provides links to state legislatures' web sites. www.ncsl.org/public/sitesleg.htm

The National League of Cities

The National League of Cities provides a list of states and for each state links to state-level Leagues of Cities. These, in turn, can help you identify your particular city. www.nlc.org

Public Technology

Public Technology offers PTILinks, which connect to state, county, and city sites. www.pti.nw.dc.us

State and Local Government on the Net

State and Local Government on the Net is a Piper Resources Guide to government-sponsored web sites. It provides links to states, counties, and cities. www.piperinfo.com

Find out how much information is available for your area. Build on this web site information by calling key officials and asking to be put on the mailing and e-mail lists for regular governmental publications that provide information and coverage of public policy issues and activities.

Index

More results-oriented books from the Amherst H. Wilder Foundation

Collaboration

Collaboration Handbook
Creating, Sustaining, and Enjoying the Journey
by Michael Winer and Karen Ray

Shows you how to get a collaboration going, set goals, determine everyone's roles, create an action plan, and evaluate the results. Includes a case study of one collaboration from start to finish, helpful tips on how to avoid pitfalls, and worksheets to keep everyone on track.

192 pages, softcover   Item # 069032

Collaboration: What Makes It Work, 2nd Ed.
by Paul Mattessich, PhD, Marta Murray-Close, BA, and Barbara Monsey, MPH

An in-depth review of current collaboration research. Major findings are summarized, critical conclusions are drawn, and twenty key factors influencing successful collaborations are identified. Includes The Wilder Collaboration Factors Inventory, which groups can use to assess their collaboration.

104 pages, softcover   Item # 069326

The Nimble Collaboration
Fine-Tuning Your Collaboration for Lasting Success
by Karen Ray

Shows you ways to make your existing collaboration more responsive, flexible, and productive. Provides three key strategies to help your collaboration respond quickly to changing environments and participants.

136 pages, softcover   Item # 069288

Funder's Guides

Community Visions, Community Solutions
Grantmaking for Comprehensive Impact
by Joseph A. Connor and Stephanie Kadel-Taras

Helps foundations, community funds, government agencies, and other grantmakers uncover a community's highest aspiration for itself, and support and sustain strategic efforts to get to workable solutions.

128 pages, softcover   Item # 06930X

Strengthening Nonprofit Performance
A Funder's Guide to Capacity Building
Paul Connolly and Carol Lukas

This practical guide synthesizes the most recent capacity building practice and research into a collection of strategies, steps, and examples that you can use to get started on or improve funding to strengthen nonprofit organizations.

176 pages, softcover   Item # 069377

Management & Planning

The Best of the Board Café
Hands-on Solutions for Nonprofit Boards
by Jan Masaoka, CompassPoint Nonprofit Services

Gathers the most requested articles from the e-newsletter, *Board Café*. You'll find a lively menu of ideas, information, opinions, news, and resources to help board members give and get the most out of their board service.

232 pages, softcover   Item # 069407

Bookkeeping Basics
What Every Nonprofit Bookkeeper Needs to Know
by Debra L. Ruegg and Lisa M. Venkatrathnam

Complete with step-by-step instructions, a glossary of accounting terms, detailed examples, and handy reproducible forms, this book will enable you to successfully meet the basic bookkeeping requirements of your nonprofit organization—even if you have little or no formal accounting training.

128 pages, softcover   Item # 069296

Consulting with Nonprofits: A Practitioner's Guide
by Carol A. Lukas

A step-by-step, comprehensive guide for consultants. Addresses the art of consulting, how to run your business, and much more. Also includes tips and anecdotes from thirty skilled consultants.

240 pages, softcover   Item # 069172

For current prices or to order visit us online at www.wilder.org/pubs

The Wilder Nonprofit Field Guide to
Crafting Effective Mission and Vision Statements
by Emil Angelica

Guides you through two six-step processes that result in a mission statement, vision statement, or both. Shows how a clarified mission and vision lead to more effective leadership, decisions, fundraising, and management. Includes tips, sample statements, and worksheets.

88 pages, softcover   Item # 06927X

The Wilder Nonprofit Field Guide to
Developing Effective Teams
by Beth Gilbertsen and Vijit Ramchandani

Helps you understand, start, and maintain a team. Provides tools and techniques for writing a mission statement, setting goals, conducting effective meetings, creating ground rules to manage team dynamics, making decisions in teams, creating project plans, and developing team spirit.

80 pages, softcover   Item # 069202

The Five Life Stages of Nonprofit Organizations
Where You Are, Where You're Going, and What to Expect When You Get There
by Judith Sharken Simon with J. Terence Donovan

Shows you what's "normal" for each development stage which helps you plan for transitions, stay on track, and avoid unnecessary struggles. Includes The Wilder Nonprofit Life Stage Assessment to plot your organization's progress in seven arenas of organization development.

128 pages, softcover   Item # 069229

The Lobbying and Advocacy Handbook for Nonprofit Organizations
Shaping Public Policy at the State and Local Level
by Marcia Avner

The Lobbying and Advocacy Handbook is a planning guide and resource for nonprofit organizations that want to influence issues that matter to them. This book will help you decide whether to lobby and then put plans in place to make it work.

240 pages, softcover   Item # 069261

The Manager's Guide to Program Evaluation:
Planning, Contracting, and Managing for Useful Results
by Paul W. Mattessich, Ph.D.

Explains how to plan and manage an evaluation that will help identify your organization's successes, share information with key audiences, and improve services.

96 pages, softcover   Item # 069385

The Nonprofit Board Member's Guide to Lobbying and Advocacy
by Marcia Avner

Written specifically for board members, this guide helps organizations increase their impact on policy decisions. It reveals how board members can be involved in planning for and implementing successful lobbying efforts.

126 pages, softcover   Item # 069393

The Nonprofit Mergers Workbook
The Leader's Guide to Considering, Negotiating, and Executing a Merger
by David La Piana

A merger can be a daunting and complex process. Save time, money, and untold frustration with this highly practical guide that makes the process manageable and controllable. Includes case studies, decision trees, twenty-two worksheets, checklists, tips, and complete step-by-step guidance from seeking partners to writing the merger agreement, and more.

240 pages, softcover   Item # 069210

The Nonprofit Mergers Workbook Part II
Unifying the Organization after a Merger
by La Piana Associates

Once the merger agreement is signed, the question becomes: How do we make this merger work? *Part II* helps you create a comprehensive plan to achieve *integration*—bringing together people, programs, processes, and systems from two (or more) organizations into a single, unified whole.

248 pages, includes CD-ROM   Item # 069415

For current prices, a catalog, or to order call ☎ 800-274-6024

Resolving Conflict in Nonprofit Organizations
The Leader's Guide to Finding Constructive Solutions
by Marion Peters Angelica

Helps you identify conflict, decide whether to intervene, uncover and deal with the true issues, and design and conduct a conflict resolution process. Includes exercises to learn and practice conflict resolution skills, guidance on handling unique conflicts such as harassment and discrimination, and when (and where) to seek outside help with litigation, arbitration, and mediation.

192 pages, softcover   Item # 069164

Strategic Planning Workbook for Nonprofit Organizations, Revised and Updated
by Bryan Barry

Chart a wise course for your nonprofit's future. This time-tested workbook gives you practical step-by-step guidance, real-life examples, one nonprofit's complete strategic plan, and easy-to-use worksheets.

144 pages, softcover   Item # 069075

Marketing & Fundraising

The Wilder Nonprofit Field Guide to
Conducting Successful Focus Groups
by Judith Sharken Simon

Shows how to collect valuable information without a lot of money or special expertise. Using this proven technique, you'll get essential opinions and feedback to help you check out your assumptions, do better strategic planning, improve services or products, and more.

80 pages, softcover   Item # 069199

Coping with Cutbacks:
The Nonprofit Guide to Success When Times Are Tight
by Emil Angelica and Vincent Hyman

Shows you practical ways to involve business, government, and other nonprofits to solve problems together. Also includes 185 cutback strategies you can put to use right away.

128 pages, softcover   Item # 069091

The Wilder Nonprofit Field Guide to
Fundraising on the Internet
by Gary M. Grobman, Gary B. Grant, and Steve Roller

Your quick road map to using the Internet for fundraising. Shows you how to attract new donors, troll for grants, get listed on sites that assist donors, and learn more about the art of fundraising. Includes detailed reviews of 77 web sites useful to fundraisers, including foundations, charities, prospect research sites, and sites that assist donors.

64 pages, softcover   Item # 069180

Marketing Workbook for Nonprofit Organizations Volume I: Develop the Plan
by Gary J. Stern

Don't just wish for results—get them! Here's how to create a straightforward, usable marketing plan. Includes the six Ps of Marketing, how to use them effectively, a sample marketing plan, tips on using the Internet, and worksheets.

208 pages, softcover   Item # 069253

Marketing Workbook for Nonprofit Organizations Volume II: Mobilize People for Marketing Success
by Gary J. Stern

Put together a successful promotional campaign based on the most persuasive tool of all: personal contact. Learn how to mobilize your entire organization, its staff, volunteers, and supporters in a focused, one-to-one marketing campaign. Comes with *Pocket Guide for Marketing Representatives*. In it, your marketing representatives can record key campaign messages and find motivational reminders.

192 pages, softcover   Item # 069105

Venture Forth! The Essential Guide to Starting a Moneymaking Business in Your Nonprofit Organization
by Rolfe Larson

The most complete guide on nonprofit business development. Building on the experience of dozens of organizations, this handbook gives you a time-tested approach for finding, testing, and launching a successful nonprofit business venture.

272 pages, softcover   Item # 069245

For current prices or to order visit us online at www.wilder.org/pubs

Vital Communities

Community Building: What Makes It Work
by Wilder Research Center

Reveals twenty-eight keys to help you build community more effectively. Includes detailed descriptions of each factor, case examples of how they play out, and practical questions to assess your work.

112 pages, softcover   Item # 069121

Community Economic Development Handbook
by Mihailo Temali

A concrete, practical handbook to turning any neighborhood around. It explains how to start a community economic development organization, and then lays out the steps of four proven and powerful strategies for revitalizing inner-city neighborhoods.

288 pages, softcover   Item # 069369

The Wilder Nonprofit Field Guide to
Conducting Community Forums
by Carol Lukas and Linda Hoskins

Provides step-by-step instruction to plan and carry out exciting, successful community forums that will educate the public, build consensus, focus action, or influence policy.

128 pages, softcover   Item # 069318

ORDERING INFORMATION

Order by phone, fax or online

 Call toll-free: 800-274-6024
Internationally: 651-659-6024

 Fax: 651-642-2061

 E-mail: books@wilder.org
Online: www.wilder.org/pubs

 Mail: Amherst H. Wilder Foundation
Publishing Center
919 Lafond Avenue
St. Paul, MN 55104

Our NO-RISK guarantee

If you aren't completely satisfied with any book for any reason, simply send it back within 30 days for a full refund.

Pricing and discounts

For current prices and discounts, please visit our web site at www.wilder.org/pubs or call toll free at 800-274-6024.

Do you have a book idea?

Wilder Publishing Center seeks manuscripts and proposals for books in the fields of nonprofit management and community development. To get a copy of our author guidelines, please call us at 800-274-6024. You can also download them from our web site at www.wilder.org/pubs/author_guide.html.

Visit us online

You'll find information about the Wilder Foundation and more details on our books, such as table of contents, pricing, discounts, endorsements, and more, at www.wilder.org/pubs.

Quality assurance

We strive to make sure that all the books we publish are helpful and easy to use. Our major workbooks are tested and critiqued by experts before being published. Their comments help shape the final book and—we trust—make it more useful to you.